Things
Left
Unsaid

Things Left Unsaid

My Dad, the Mob, and Growing Up in the Nevada Gaming Industry

Glenn E. Wichinsky

Published by GFB™, Seattle
www.girlfridayproductions.com

Produced by Girl Friday Productions

Design: Paul Barrett
Production editorial: Katherine Richards
Project management: Sara Addicott

Image credits: cover © Shutterstock/WildSnap

ISBN (paperback): 978-1-967510-19-1
ISBN (ebook): 978-1-967510-20-7

Library of Congress Control Number: 2025919706

First edition

To my father, who once reflected that he had lived a full life and now enjoyed helping others.

Contents

Prologue

My father, Michael "Mickey" Wichinsky, passed away in February 2013 at the age of ninety. I had known and loved my father for the man he was, his strengths and shortcomings as a father included. I knew him from afar, as my parents divorced when I was just four years old. I grew up on the East Coast with my mother and two siblings, while my father seemed to be living an intriguing life in Las Vegas, Nevada. He was a hotel and casino executive at the Sands Hotel, during a time when the hotels and casinos on the Las Vegas Strip were mostly owned, operated, and controlled by the various families involved in organized crime across the United States. There are so many questions I wish I had asked him about his life, but he always seemed reluctant to delve into the past. We never discussed his childhood, his stories of growing up, whether he played any sports or had any hobbies, or his experience being married to my mother and starting a family at a young age.

It wasn't until three months after his passing, when I purchased a copy of the book *Hit Me! Fighting the Las Vegas Mob by the Numbers* by Danielle Gomes and Jay Bonansinga, that I began to learn the true story about the life my father had led. He was involved with individuals who were associated with organized crime, and he chose not to fully share this life with me for my own protection. Reading Gomes and Bonansinga's book provided a clearer focus on my father's prior life and activities, making me rethink everything I had experienced with him. I needed to find out what had truly transpired during my father's secretive life.

"If you don't say anything, you won't get in trouble."

My father shared these poignant words with me many times over the years. This credo that he lived by—for both his physical and financial survival while working at the Sands during the 1950s and '60s—was a concept of constant strategic thinking and self-editing. I also employed this mindset in making many important decisions for my own success and personal survival.

CHAPTER 1

My Family Roots

Maybe it was fate that my father would end up working in the casino business, considering he grew up in Hurleyville, New York. It was a quiet little town in the foothills of the Catskill Mountains, but it was also a place with a dark history of crime that contradicted its quaint, small-town image.

When I grew up there in the 1950s, Hurleyville had a population of about five hundred residents in the winter and eight hundred in the summer. The area was known as a retreat for many Jewish families who desired to leave the hot and steamy streets of New York City in the summer. It was a place of fresh air, renewed youth, fishing, and berry picking where you could make and maintain summertime friendships at the many bungalow colonies and small hotels in the region. The year-round residents lived through the warmth of summer but also the blizzards and indoor seclusion of the long, frigid winters. Until I was four, my family and I lived in Hurleyville throughout the year. There was my father; my mother, Ann; and my siblings, Steven and Claudia, who were eight and five years older than me, respectively. We lived on Main Street in a house that, some years earlier, was the home of the *Hurleyville Sentinel* newspaper.

My parents met and married in the Catskills toward the end of World War II. My father was the youngest of nine children who mostly raised each other in very small living quarters situated above the family bakery. Their father, Jacob—whom we called Grandpa Jake—had a checkered history as a husband and businessman, and their mother, Ida, was either voluntarily admitted or committed to a state institution shortly after the birth of my father, possibly due to the abuse and oppression by her husband.

I didn't know my grandfather very well as I was only seven years old when he passed away. I heard many stories about him and his character, none of which were complimentary. An article published in the local newspaper during the 1930s told a story of Grandpa Jake engaging in an argument with Grandma Ida and how he proceeded to threaten her with an axe. When the Hurleyville Town Council was informed of the incident, they voted to have Grandpa Jake expelled from the village. He stayed away from Hurleyville and his family for some time until he was able to convince the town council that his presence was essential for the continued successful operation of the family bakery.

My earliest recollection of him is seeing him seated in a rocking chair on the sidewalk in front of the bakery, with his large round spectacles and wearing a white baker's smock. He would sit there and smoke his pipe while gazing across Main Street.

My cousin Julian once told me he noticed that none of the family had named their children after our grandpa following his passing in 1959. So he decided to name his dog Jake.

Hurleyville was composed of small businesses, farms, and boardinghouses in a very rural setting. Visitors to Hurleyville and its neighboring villages in the Catskills would either arrive in town on the O&W Railway (which the locals referred to as the "Old and Weary") at the Hurleyville train station or drive a hundred miles by car from New York City. The latter is how my mother's family arrived in town.

My maternal grandfather, Louis Pesekow, was a barber by trade who emigrated from Russia to the United States at the turn of the century. He had served in the Russian cavalry in czarist times but deserted, fleeing from a life of emotional pain and oppression that he and his family experienced during the antisemitic rule of Czar Nicholas II. He escaped from his military service by hiding in a horse cart covered with hay and eventually made his way across Europe to Holland. He was seeking a new life in America and the chance to join some of his brothers and sisters who had already immigrated there.

Grandpa Louis left Holland on an ocean vessel with mostly just the clothes on his back. However, he was so successful at engaging in marathon card games during the three-week transatlantic journey that he accumulated enough winnings to begin his new life in the United States. Once he was settled in the country, he opened and operated his first barbershop in Brooklyn, New York. He was a hard worker and saved his profits to—as he said—"own a piece of America" as well as support his new wife, Ethel, and their family, which later consisted of four children. He purchased a mixed-use building of residential rooms at 447 Herzl Street in the Brownsville section of Brooklyn. The upstairs became the family living quarters, and the ground floor had commercial units. One of the commercial units was leased out for the operation of a neighborhood grocery store.

My grandfather was an entrepreneur who lived life to the fullest. While he was a dedicated worker and high achiever during the workweek, he also enjoyed going fishing and spending an occasional weekend day at the Monticello Raceway, placing bets on the various horse races. In fact, he loved horses so much that when I was a child he once encouraged me to become a jockey. I was short and quite small for my age in my early years. Unfortunately, I was afraid of horses, so I had to turn him down.

Sometime in the early 1930s, Louis and Ethel decided to spend their summers in upstate New York. They came to Loch Sheldrake, which was a small township situated along beautiful Loch Sheldrake Lake. They located a rental property bordering the lake that consisted of ten cottages, also known as bungalows. They originally rented these cottages from the owner of the property and then re-rented most of them to other families looking to escape New York City in the summer. It was a journey of a hundred miles to Loch Sheldrake from Brooklyn, but always a time of happiness and celebration for my mother and her siblings—another wonderful summer with family members and new and old tenants who eventually became close friends over the years.

By the time I was growing up, Hurleyville hadn't changed all that much. It was such a small town that if you called someone local by phone it was not unlikely for the switchboard operator to tell you the person you were trying to reach was at someone else's house playing cards. She would then redirect the call.

On the west side of Main Street walking north from our house was a small fish market, a hardware store, Jacobson's butcher shop, Wood's Studio, and Bockman's Pharmacy. The east side of Main Street consisted of a synagogue, the Sullivan Dairy, Wichinsky's Bake Shop, and Perk's Market. Farther up Main Street were Ernie's Bar (a local hangout reputedly also known for its brothel on the second floor), a barbershop, Freier's Luncheonette, another bar, and other small businesses.

The business owners were colorful in their own way. Abe

Jacobson, the butcher, had a wonderful and friendly personality coupled with a booming voice.

"How are you, Pressure Pete?" he would shout out to me. I figured I got the nickname due to my less than overwhelming handshake as a child.

There was Dave Bockman, who owned the drugstore and was a pharmacist by occupation. In addition to operating the store as a pharmacy and luncheon counter, he sold household appliances. Dave was also a ham radio operator, and his love for shortwave radio influenced me in later years. His call sign as he would announce on the air was "W2TUP, T—Tom, U—Union, P—Peter."

We bought our first black-and-white television from Dave. I would turn on our small TV set and try to direct the rabbit-ear antennas to gain a clearer signal from the closest television station, which was broadcasting a hundred miles away in New York City. Sometimes I could watch my cartoons and other favorite shows if I could receive a viewable television program through a strong broadcasting signal. It was not unusual for new TV owners to encase their television antennas with aluminum foil in a compressed oval shape at the extended ends to improve video reception. It was still worth watching our favorite cartoons, even if the reception was weak. In later years, broadcast transmitting repeaters were placed above Columbia Hill, just south of Hurleyville, which enhanced television reception for the nearby villages.

Perky of Perk's Market was the local grocer and brother to Abe, the butcher shop owner. One day, when I was an infant, my mother took me shopping at Perk's. Perky called my mother through the local switchboard operator after she and I left the grocery store.

"Hello, Annie, it was nice to see you and little Glenn at my store today."

"It was nice to see you too, Perky," my mother replied.

"I thought you might find it funny to know that after you and Glenn left, I noticed that most of my apples in the bin had small teeth marks in them. Teeth marks from, say, a little boy about Glenn's age."

Horrified, my mother apologized profusely. "He's teething and will bite anything he can get his hands on!"

"Don't worry about it, Annie," Perky replied in good humor. "See you and Glenn again soon."

Graciously, Perk didn't make my mother purchase the apples.

Hurleyville is in Sullivan County. During the 1930s and into the 1940s, this area was also known as a dumping ground for those who were "hit" by the Mob through their enforcement arm known as Murder, Inc. Mob activities were orchestrated and directed by such famous mobsters as Meyer Lansky and Bugsy Siegel. Organized crime families were very active in New York City and New Jersey in this era, and they engaged in many illicit criminal activities, including murder.

Whenever someone created problems for the Mob or got out of line, they would often be found either buried in a lime pit in the Catskills or floating in Loch Sheldrake Lake or nearby Swan Lake. There are many stories about this in the 1930s and into the mid-1940s. One day, two children went into town to speak to the local police chief after rowing a boat on the lake. They innocently stated they had noticed a man playing a pinball machine in the middle of the lake. The police investigated and found another victim of Murder, Inc. His body was tied down to a pinball machine, but it hadn't sunk and was floating on the surface of the water. This wasn't the only time pinball or slot machines were used to attempt to sink the victims' bodies into the deep lake bed.

One year, when my mother was growing up, her sister Eleanor was in a rowboat on Loch Sheldrake Lake with her boyfriend. While rowing, they saw what they thought was a mannequin floating near their boat. As they got closer, they realized it wasn't a mannequin at all. It turned out to be a mobster who was taken out by the Mob for not playing by their established rules. He had several bullet holes in him, but his body did not sink into obscurity under the surface as intended.

There were rumors that sometimes our family bakery truck was loaned to these Mob enforcers by my father's older brother, Nate, to facilitate late-night deliveries of victims to the area. It was unclear whether Uncle Nate may have had a closer relationship with these Mob enforcers.

One of the Mob enforcers was a local Hurleyville man named Jack Drucker, who lived on a nearby farm with his family. Jack had once been given orders by the Mob bosses to execute an associate who was assigned to oversee the illegal slot machine operations in the area and who was apparently helping himself to some of the proceeds. As detailed by John Conway, author of *Muskrats, Milkmaids and Mobsters: A Brief History of Hurleyville, Vol. 1*, this individual was executed and found buried in Drucker's barn, sprinkled with lime to distort the condition of his body and make personal identification more difficult. On another occasion, according to our family friend Myron Sugerman, author of *The Chronicles of the Last Jewish Gangster: From Meyer to Myron*, Mr. Drucker attached a slot machine to one of his Mob-ordered victims, deposited him in Loch Sheldrake Lake, and told him to enjoy the swim.

Jack Drucker was arrested years later following the testimony of a few of the other criminals involved who had turned state's evidence against him. He ultimately lived out the rest of his life in prison as a convicted murderer.

These types of criminal activities continued for many years in the Catskills until, with advances in forensic science, law enforcement was able to begin solving many of these murder mysteries.

The lake had connections to my mother's family history too. One summer in the late 1930s, Grandpa Louis was approached by the owners of the cottage property with an offer to sell him the property and the cottages. The owners, Sam and Anna Tannenbaum, were in a dire financial position. They owned the lakeside property and cottages as well as the Loch Sheldrake Country Club on the adjoining property.

The country club, also known as "the Casino," was frequented by many of the diverse personalities of the time. There were locals and Mob figures from Murder, Inc. who would often drop by. One new member of the Mob was Mr. Tannenbaum's son, Al, who was later better recognized by his nickname, "Tick-Tock" Tannenbaum. Tick-Tock was very much involved as an enforcer in criminal activities on behalf of the Mob.

One evening, the Casino burned down to the ground. It could have been accidental, Mob initiated, or a case of Jewish lightning. "Jewish lightning" was a derogatory term often used to describe the intentional destruction of property that appeared accidental in order to collect the insurance monies for the value of the property. There were a few known cases of this in the Catskills at the time. As Mr. Tannenbaum did not have property insurance on the Casino, it is doubtful he set fire to his own property. Since he was then in dire need of cash, he decided to sell to Grandpa Louis the adjacent property and cottages for a much-needed sum of $10,000.

Most residents and businesspeople in Loch Sheldrake were aware of how the Mob members conducted their business, and they were careful in how they interacted with them. Grandpa Louis was the local barber, and he would provide haircuts and shaves to the mobsters. My grandfather would try to make light of the situation when a mobster was in his barber chair. Grandpa Louis would take out his straightedge razor for shaving, place it under the neck of the mobster, and sarcastically say, "Who's the boss?" Their reply would be: "You are, Louie!"

Murder, Inc. would eventually leave the Catskills by the mid-1940s and cease to exist as a distinct criminal organization, but their principals and some former members then focused their attention on expanding their criminal activities to hotels and casinos in Cuba and later Las Vegas.

The cold and empty winters of the Catskills were often punctuated by card games, heavy drinking, cigarette smoking, and often acts of adultery. While many of the residents conducted their businesses to support the needs of the local community year-round, other business owners whose revenues were generated mostly during the summer season would temporarily move to Florida or other warmer locations to seek employment to support their families during the offseason.

Upon Grandpa Jake's passing and with Grandma Ida residing in the Middletown State Hospital, their children were on their own. I assume that some families whose incomes were largely generated only seasonally in the Catskills, like a small family bakery, might also engage in gray areas of business or illegal activities in order to make ends meet.

My father and his siblings did whatever they could to make a living and developed their own "confidential code of conduct" to abide by within the family and in the operation of the various family businesses. For example, the bake shop, which was operated by some of the siblings, was a gathering place where business affairs would be discussed. A family member, such as a spouse or child, could be visiting in the retail area of the bakery, but if important family business was to be conducted, the spouse or child would be left out front while the Wichinsky inner circle would retire behind a door leading to the back kitchen area. It was offensive to be at the receiving end of this exclusionary policy, while at the same time somewhat intriguing to ponder what was being so secretly discussed.

My father's main job was his pinball machine and jukebox route operation. He kept a storage unit and office answering machine in an adjoining room in the bakery building. The pinball machines and jukeboxes were serviced and maintained there by my father and operated seasonally at numerous businesses in the vicinity.

Not all the electronic game machines on the route operation were legal. One evening in 1944, prior to their marriage, my mother and father were on a date. My father had informed my mother that he needed to make a business stop at one of the hotels in order to hide one of the slot machines in a commercial refrigerator. Apparently, someone had tipped off my family of a planned law enforcement inspection on the hotel property. I don't know whether the Wichinsky family owned and operated these illegal slot machines or whether they only provided service to maintain the slot machines for another owner. Was my family maintaining the service and support of these slot machines for elements of the Mob? Illegal gambling activities were definitely part of the business enterprises of the Mob families in New York and New Jersey, and slot machines were tacitly operated in many of the resort hotels in the Catskills region.

During my early years, my father purchased pinball machines and jukeboxes from game distributors in New York and New Jersey for placement at various hotels, bars, and bungalow colonies. These business activities would require my father to visit these locations each week during the summer and physically empty a metal coin box from each device for accounting and revenue sharing. The coin boxes would contain mounds of nickels deposited by the young adults and children who enjoyed the machines.

He also carried a large black soldering gun with a spool of solder to repair broken connections in the pinball machine. He replaced glass panes as well, which were often broken by upset players banging their fists on the pinball machines.

When servicing the jukeboxes, he swapped out the records on a regular basis to provide the customer with a selection of the current popular songs and performing artists. The old jukeboxes of the day had open slots inside the clear cabinets where one would insert small vinyl records known as 45s. When a song was selected, a metal loading arm would mechanically move over, grasp a record from the divided storage slots, and gently place the record down onto a slowly spinning turntable for play. The tension of the arm had to be adjusted correctly, otherwise the jukebox arm would grasp the selected record, move it over the turntable, and smash it to pieces on the surface of the turntable. My father kept extra copies of the records available in case this happened.

After collecting the money from all the machines, my father would sit across a table from the location owner, and with his first and second fingers, count the coins by twos and place them into paper coin wrappers. Once all the coins were wrapped, they were stacked up and equally divided between the location owner and my father. The daily operation of the pinball machine and jukebox route was how my family made a living in the summer, with any profits realized having to last us through the frigid winter.

My father had four brothers who engaged in various legitimate and illegitimate business pursuits. Louis (Uncle Lebel) was a wonderful, free-spirited inventor. He created the automated bagel machine and a vegetable-oil-powered automobile. He also involved himself in many other notable global causes, including his support, assistance, and engagement in activities leading to the establishment of the State of Israel. Stanley owned and operated a bus company composed of a fleet of buses used for school transportation and chartered events.

Sidney carried on with the trade of their father and managed the actual bakery production until it eventually closed. The bakery made very fine bread and other baked goods. Sometimes, a rat would eat into a loaf of baked bread before the products would be brought up from the downstairs factory. Often the bread would then be cut in half, and the untouched half would be sold as a "half loaf special." The front window of the bakery displayed fruit Danish, cookies, and other pastries. It was a time when food items were not refrigerated, and long fly strips hung from the ceiling over the food to catch flies, hopefully before they landed on the open baked goods. The health departments of today would have a major problem with such practices.

Nate, the oldest son, had a demeanor very much like that of the late 1930s actor Edward G. Robinson, who always played a sinister character involved in illegal activities and exuded a sly and inviting smile. Nate was a father figure to my father but never married nor had a family of his own. He appeared to be assisting the Wichinsky family in overseeing the daily bakery operations during the summer and often claimed, when asked, that he was the owner of the bakery. He spent his winters in Miami Beach, pursuing his own personal business activities.

My father also had an older sister named Rebecca (Ricky), who was a mother figure to him and was the bookkeeper at the family bakery. Ricky had a firm grasp of the business and money. I would see her working at her rolltop desk next to the large safe at the back of the bakery floor, beyond the showcase of breads, cookies, and pastries baked each day. My mother liked Ricky but told me that she had dollar signs in her eyes instead of pupils.

My father had two other sisters, Frieda and Pauline, the latter with whom he was extremely close. Frieda was married to a land surveyor in Hurleyville and lived on a farm and cottage property on Columbia Hill, just south of the center of town. She lived the life of a dedicated wife who mostly tended to their garden and pets and was also an avid fishing enthusiast. Pauline was a beautiful young woman when she met her future husband, Don Petrin, from West Orange, New Jersey. Uncle Don was a professional light heavyweight fighter and an Italian Catholic. When Pauline married Don, Uncle Nate would no longer speak to her because she married outside the Jewish faith.

I remember Uncle Don and Aunt Pauline very well. I visited them often after we moved to New York City. Don was no longer a fighter by that time; he suffered from Parkinson's disease, possibly as a result of his career. When he walked through the neighborhoods of West Orange, the neighbors would call out to him by saying: "Hey, Champ!" Pauline was a devoted wife, raising her own children, grandchildren, and the children of other family members at times. I recall many home-cooked Italian dinners, which often featured large cheese ravioli.

My parents' marriage of twelve years ended in 1957. What began as a deeply romantic relationship with the hope of creating a long-lasting family together ended due to challenges that could not be remedied. It developed into a lonely and hurtful relationship that my mother could no longer endure. My parents' interactions at home were minimal, consisting mostly of my father complaining about migraine headaches, telling everyone to be quiet, or coming home late at night from long hours of socializing at a local bar or club. My sister, Claudia, would joke to me in later years: "You were born to save the marriage and you failed."

While my father had the financial responsibility for earning a living and raising three children, I don't believe he had the moral bandwidth necessary to nurture and maintain a traditional family life with his wife and children as a result of being raised by his father and later by his older brother and sister. Outside the Wichinsky sisters, my father did not give much respect to women as individuals and often viewed them simply in a physical sense. Their job was just to raise children and not ask any questions. My father was not a faithful husband to my mother; he lived a double life.

In the early 1950s, my father had met a woman named Betty who worked at the nearby Concord Hotel during the summers. She was divorced and had a young son, Mark. Her winter home was in New Jersey, which was about a two-hour drive from Hurleyville. She and my father developed and maintained a romantic relationship for many years and spent much time together when my father commuted from Hurleyville to New York City and New Jersey, ostensibly to conduct his business. She joined him on overseas business trips when he began engaging in the game export market, and my mother eventually became aware of his secret life through gossip whispered and shared within the small local community of Hurleyville.

Many years later, Mark and I became very well acquainted as we began sharing our own personal memories of my father based on our childhoods. Although we are not biologically connected, we consider ourselves related through our experiences with my father. We have also developed a close bond and relationship as a result and refer to each other as "Brother Glenn" and "Brother Mark." Mark once shared with me that he always thought his mother was actually married to my father. That is what he was led to believe. At one point, when Mark was in his early twenties, he was employed in the sales and marketing office of the Sands Hotel, which was just south of Central Park in the Manhattan borough of New York City. While having coffee with his boss and respective spouse, he was asked, "How are you related to Mickey?" Mark proudly stated that "Mickey is married to my mother." The spouse said, "Oh, your mother is Zola?" Mark was stunned by her remark. It was at that moment that he realized his mother had not been married to my father.

More recently, Mark told me that he and his mother had lived for a year in Monticello, New York, so that my father could be closer to his mother. Monticello was three miles from the house where I had lived in Hurleyville. I assumed that this had occurred after my parents divorced in 1957. I asked Mark to share more of this story with me and if he recalled what year this took place. Mark responded, "Mickey and my mom would occasionally ask me to join them for dinner at a nearby restaurant. The restaurant had a jukebox, and I would always select my favorite song, "The Ballad of Davy Crockett," while also wearing my Davy Crockett outfit and hat. Your dad couldn't stand listening to the song being played and pleaded with me not to play it again." I began thinking about the time-line of events and said, "Mark, when was this song released by the record companies?" He didn't know. So, at that point, I reached for my cell phone and did a Google search. To my surprise, it was released in 1955, which was a time when I was still living with my mother and my siblings in Hurleyville just a few miles away. My parents' divorce did not occur until two years later. I am thankful my mother never knew this.

My mother finally chose to end a hurtful and very lonely relationship when I was four years old. My mother, Steven, Claudia, and I then left Hurleyville and moved to New York City. For many years after their divorce, my mother could not bear to listen to the song "Auld Lang Syne" on New Year's Eve because being alone that day reminded her of the painful years of marriage to my father.

CHAPTER 2

Living in the Bronx

My mother, along with my siblings and me, relocated to the Bronx in 1957. We moved into apartment 6P on the top floor of the David Farragut Building at 1075 Grand Concourse and lived there for five years following my parents' divorce. My mother's sister, Sylvia Smith, had lived there with her own family for a couple of decades before, but following her own divorce, she moved to Florida, and we moved into the apartment under her last name and her lease. I wondered why the directory listing for apartment 6P showed us as the Smith family but learned years later that we moved in this way to secure the set rent-controlled rate of $110 per month, which had been established under Aunt Sylvia's lease.

One day, the apartment building landlord knocked on our door and my mother asked what he wanted. He showed her a mailed envelope that had arrived for her, listing her last name as Wichinsky, not Smith. He then told my mother that he now had proof that we were living in the apartment under someone else's lease. He showed her the envelope and said, "What does W-I-C-H-I-N-S-K-Y spell?"

With an equally commanding response, my mother said, "SMITH!" She then proceeded to squat down in front of the landlord, announced that she had "squatters' rights," and firmly closed the apartment door in his face. The landlord never bothered us again.

As a young child, I found living in the Bronx to be a fun time. I would walk to my elementary school on Cromwell Avenue, Public School 114. I made many friends and fielded second base on the High Bridge Little League. We played our Little League games on the field directly across the street from the old Yankee Stadium. The new and current Yankee Stadium is actually on the old Little League field that I used to play baseball on.

In school, I was the lead actor in our play production of *Cinderella*. No, I did not perform the role of Cinderella; in this version of the play, the lead was a cobbler named Mooney, who crafted the famous glass slipper for Cinderella. I memorized my lines so well that the teacher decided not to cast an understudy for my part. Then, on the day of the class play, I woke up with itchy red bumps on the midsection of my body, which my mother immediately recognized as chicken pox. She called my teacher at P.S. 114 and explained the dilemma. As the show had to go on and I had no understudy, I was instructed to come to school regardless of my medical condition to play the role of the cobbler. I performed my part to perfection, and following the applause of the audience and the closing of the curtain, I was immediately ushered off the stage and sent home with my mother.

The cast of the play was treated to a day trip to see the Statue of Liberty the next morning in appreciation for their hard work and fine performance. I, however, had to stay home for the next few days and spent my time watching cartoons and movies on TV while dabbing pink calamine lotion on each newly appearing red bump to relieve the itching. It wasn't until many years later that my mother was able to finally take me to see the Statue of Liberty.

Outside school, I learned how to play and enjoy games of stickball, curb ball, and twenty-one, in which we threw a pink Spalding ball behind the metal gratings of the windows for points. We played hide-and-seek, placing different directional arrows in chalk on the sidewalk to confuse the seekers. We also listened in wonder as we heard the roar of the crowd from Yankee Stadium whenever Roger Maris or Mickey Mantle hit a home run. I have always been a New York Yankees fan, and my favorite number is seven. Mickey Mantle, who wore number seven on his Yankee uniform, was my childhood idol.

If I wanted to walk to Emma's, a local corner store where you could buy anything from baseball cards and Spalding balls to vanilla malteds and Bonomo Turkish Taffy, I would need some money. My mother would call down to me from our sixth-floor apartment and then drop a few coins that were wrapped and taped in a tissue, and off I went.

My father had moved to Las Vegas and was working at the Sands Hotel and Casino by this time. He would occasionally visit us when he was traveling to the East Coast for business reasons. On one trip, he took me to Madison Square Garden to see the Harlem Globetrotters perform. We also used to frequent a small Chinese restaurant in Harlem. The Shanghai Cafe was under the elevated train at Broadway and 125th Street. They prepared the most fabulous Chinese food and brought out endless platters of fried dumplings. To go along with the culinary magic was their longtime, popular, and personable employee, Jimmy Zhou, whom we called Jimmy How. Jimmy was a cheerful young man who always served us our dinner. We visited the Shanghai Cafe many times over the five years I lived in the Bronx.

Some years later, as a young adult, I traveled back to the Shanghai Cafe to enjoy the offerings of the establishment once again. I was surprised when I was met at my table by this elderly man who was bald and slightly hunched over. He greeted me and my party with a very familiar smile. It was Jimmy Zhou! A few years ago, I made my way up Broadway and was sad to learn that, like most established restaurants of many years eventually do, the Shanghai Cafe had closed.

My siblings and maternal family cousins had a great interest in applied music. I believe this interest in music stemmed from the fact that my uncle, James (Jimmy) Smith, who had been married to my aunt Sylvia, led a very successful career for decades as a professional trumpet player with the New York Philharmonic, under the direction of Leonard Bernstein. My cousins became accomplished flute and trumpet players, and my sister also enjoyed learning how to play the flute at Jordan Mott Junior High 22 from her music teacher, Mr. Abraham Matus. Mr. Matus would come to our apartment to give Claudia her flute lessons. I also had an interest in learning how to play the saxophone. Once I was seven years old, when my fingers were long enough to reach around the instrument keys and my front teeth were fully in, I began to study the saxophone. I continued playing saxophone throughout my childhood and ultimately at the University of Miami School of Music.

My family had adopted my cousin Steven after his mother died and his father left him and his two sisters. From then on he was my brother. But Steven lived a different life than I did during the Bronx years. He was eight years older than me and, understandably, a troubled teenager. Steven cut his classes at Taft High School and found his way to the local pool halls. He often used his talent for changing each hand-printed "F" grade on his report cards into the letter *A* by drawing a simple diagonal line on the right side of the letter.

Once, my mother received a phone call from the high school principal offering his condolences for the loss of her father, my grandpa Louis, after Steven had missed several days of classes for this purported reason. My mother was shocked and alarmed by the phone call as her father was in very good health at the time and enjoying his life with my grandmother in North Miami, Florida.

Steven was a challenge to my mother while my father was many miles away in Las Vegas. When Steven ultimately dropped out of Taft in 1961, my mother pressured him to enlist in the US Army, which he did reluctantly.

Steven did his basic training at Fort Dix in New Jersey and later was based at Fort Hood in Killeen, Texas. While Steven was on his tour of service in the army in the early 1960s, our neighborhood in the South Bronx became unsafe with local gang elements. This was part of the reason why my mother, Claudia, and I moved to North Miami Beach in Florida in 1962. We would live near our cousins, aunts and uncles, and my maternal grandparents. My father came through for us and made this relocation and my mother's ownership of a new home possible.

One day, a federal or state law enforcement agent visited us in North Miami Beach and asked my mother where she had received the funds to buy such a nice new home.

"My father provided the funds for us to purchase the house," she said, perhaps realizing in that moment that there might be something questionable about how her ex-husband had obtained the money.

"Well then, ma'am, I am going to need to question your father. What's his name? Where can I find your father to address these questions?"

"You can find Louis Pesekow at Lakeside Memorial Park in Miami."

That was the end of that.

CHAPTER 3

Summers in the Catskills

As a child, I did not spend any time at summer camp like so many of my friends in North Miami Beach did. I was so very fortunate to spend my summers in Loch Sheldrake at the same bungalow property where my mother and her family had spent their childhood years. Whether we made the journey to the Catskills after the school year was over by driving a hundred miles from the Bronx or, in later years, driving fifteen hundred miles from South Florida, the month of June was a cherished time for me. When the school year was over and I was promoted to the next grade, my mother would pack up our car and we would head to Pesekow's Bungalow Colony. We had a wonderful small bungalow next door to my mom's brother, Uncle Iggy, and it was just up the hill from the Casino on the shoreline of Loch Sheldrake Lake.

The front of the bungalow had a small porch facing the sidewalk expanses of the bungalow property. We had a new kitchen that my grandfather had built for us and beyond that was a small living area that held three twin-sized beds for me,

Claudia, and my mother. By this time, Steven no longer lived with us. The bathroom reminded me of an airplane lavatory in size and amenity. There was a shower with barely enough room to stand in and a very small sink that, when used, would leave us with water running down our elbows and creating small puddles on the floor.

On clear summer days we could see the sun rise from between the roof and the interior wall of the bungalow. This was not the intended design of the bungalow when it was built in 1938, but the result of the dilapidated condition of the building after many years of harsh winter weather and natural decay. Small branches from a beautiful pine tree attempted to gain entry through the opening in the structure. During heavy rainstorms we would run to the kitchen and get pots and pans to place along the floor in the bedroom area to catch the rain coming in through the middle seam of our roof, which was not sealed properly. We were never nervous or worried at all. It was just part of our yearly summer adventure.

We lived economically off the $500 monthly alimony payment that my father sent. While $500 was worth much more in the 1960s than it is today, it still didn't leave us much to live on when our mortgage payment on our home in North Miami Beach was $125 each month. My mother always placed her children first, and we had all the essentials. To make ends meet during the summer, my mother worked in her brother Iggy's beauty shop in Loch Sheldrake, shampooing clients' hair.

Most summer days began with my mother getting up early in the morning, walking into town, and working for her small salary and tips. Before she left, she prepared breakfast for me and left a loving note on the kitchen table. Breakfast was usually some cold cereal to add milk to and a bagel with cream cheese and jelly. She placed a small bowl on top of the food to keep the flies away. She would also leave me a quarter so I could play five games on the pinball machine in the Casino. So I started the day by having my breakfast, placing the quarter in my pocket for later, and then looking for my friends who were also regulars at the bungalow colony every summer.

There was such a wonderful variety of things to do each day. I could go swimming in the large pool on the property on a warm day, or I could take a rowboat out on Loch Sheldrake Lake and visit the shallow, marshy area known as Chinaman's Alley. It was a mysterious place for us to explore, same as it had been for my mother and her siblings during their youth.

Some days my friends wanted to play games of punchball, stickball, or handball on the handball court. I practiced my pitching skills early in the morning before stickball games, doing my windup and pitch with a pink rubber Spalding ball against the handball court wall, where a pitching or strike box had previously been painted. I became good at throwing fastballs, curveballs, screwballs, and a pitch we used to call a crossfire. I really enjoyed our games, even though I was one of the younger kids and not always invited to play with the "big kids."

Some days we went berry picking for wild strawberries, raspberries, and blueberries. Before he passed, Grandpa Louis used to love strawberries, and he would make me feel ten feet tall when I picked the small, wild strawberries from the hill behind Bungalow #9 and ran to the Casino to give them to him. My grandmother would add some sour cream with a dash of sugar on top, and my grandfather was so happy to eat what was prepared for him.

The Casino had a food concession area that my grandparents would operate every summer. There was a counter with traditional rotating red diner stools, and you could buy anything—candy, sodas, frozen chocolate marshmallow twists, baseball cards, gum. They also served freshly prepared pizza by the slice. Most of the bungalow colony summer residents did not carry money during the day, so a whiteboard was situated behind the door to the concession area with a column of charges accrued for each guest. Their bill would be brought current by the end of each month. I was fortunate and privileged not to have an account because I was "Pesekow's grandson." This meant that I would have an open and free account to choose anything I wanted at any time from the concession. My grandmother would always say to me in Yiddish, *"Komm, kind, ess,"* meaning "Come, child, eat." My favorites at the Casino were the frozen chocolate and marshmallow twists, which we called frozen twists, and Orange Crush soda.

One day, I went fishing for the first time. We used worms we found at night, called night crawlers, and placed them on the fishing line hook as bait. I was so excited the very first time I caught a small fish on my fishing pole. It turned out to be a sunfish, which we called sunnies. My grandfather was with me, and he gently took the fish off the hook. He wanted to make his grandson feel special, so he cleaned the fish and prepared gefilte fish, which is a Jewish delicacy consisting of poached fish dumplings.

Our other summertime childhood adventures spanned from catching orange salamanders under the dense trees, catching fireflies and placing them in glass jars with vented tops, and playing Michigan Rummy and other card games for pennies in the Casino.

By our teenage years, we had graduated to listening to the jukebox, watching movies that were projected on a large screen inside the Casino on select evenings, and experiencing our first dates. When I was thirteen, I met a girl named Sandy who came to the bungalow colony one summer to visit her grandparents. She had long brown hair parted on the side and would listen to the music playing on the jukebox and engage in a dance she called the Boston Monkey. I got the courage to ask her out on a date, and we both walked into town to the

Strand Theater to see the movie *A Patch of Blue*, starring actor Sidney Poitier. We enjoyed the film, and after walking back to the bungalow colony, I had my first kiss behind Bungalow #7.

We all spent many evenings around the bonfire near the lake, sharing stories while roasting marshmallows stuck on long tree branches. In addition to our bonfires, probably the greatest event of the entire summer was the Fourth of July, when we would set off fireworks from the handball court to celebrate Independence Day. We had an assortment of bottle rockets, which we would aim and shoot up and across the lakeshore in an informal competition with those who lived on the other side of the lake. We also enjoyed Black Cat firecrackers, cherry bombs, ash cans, and M-80s, which were mostly set off by the big kids.

Twice during the summer, the families would gather in the Casino for an evening event sponsored by my grandparents. There was live music, including an accordion player performing Yiddish and ethnic tunes, and my grandfather would dance the Russian *kazatske* while balancing a glass of water on his forehead. Large spreads of different types of prepared fish and cold cuts were provided, and the festivities lasted for hours. Typically, by nine, the children were sent back to their bungalows for the evening and the party continued for adults only. The ongoing laughter, music, and loud conversations traveled through the calm and cool evening air and up through my window, reaching me in bed.

There was also a large deck adjoining the Casino. From there, we often gazed out into the evening stars—a treat since there were no streetlights to restrict our view of the galaxy. One summer night, we watched in amazement at the overhead passing of the Russian satellite Sputnik. The big kids spent time in the secluded rear portion of the Casino's deck, engaging in romantic pursuits and carving their names into the back wall for posterity.

When I was eleven years old, my uncle Iggy gave me my first job working at his beauty shop. I was given a large industrial push broom, and it was my responsibility to sweep all the hair off the beauty shop floor. I would be paid fifty cents each weekend and, occasionally, I also earned tips from the customers.

The beauty shop had a bank of old-fashioned hair dryers that, when in use, made the women seem to have coneheads. It was hot in the summer heat and even hotter under the hair dryers. One day, a beauty shop customer named Mildred asked me to walk across the street to the luncheon counter at Sakofsky's drugstore to purchase a vanilla shake for her. So I did that for her, and she was so pleased she thanked me by handing me a dollar. I often ran errands for people at the shop, and it was nice spending more time with my mother and sister while they were also working there. Claudia liked the sour pickles from Joe's Delicatessen, a few doors down, so I often bought her a pickle for five cents and had it wrapped in a napkin so she could easily hold it while eating.

The summers seemed to fly by, and by mid-August I felt a general sense of sadness, realizing that another summer was about to end. We packed up the car before Labor Day weekend, said goodbye to our summertime friends, and promised to keep in touch with each other. My deepest hope was that everyone would come back again next summer and for many more summers to come. But Labor Day meant it was time to go back home and begin another school year.

CHAPTER 4

New Life in North Miami Beach

We moved to North Miami Beach from the Bronx at the end of another wonderful summer vacation in Loch Sheldrake in 1962. It felt like a transition from the frantic life of the city into the country. The home my father helped us buy was a three-bedroom, two-bath house on 179th Street in a safe and quiet middle-class neighborhood.

The day after we settled into the new house, I saw some boys my age playing baseball out front using a tennis ball instead of a baseball. This was done so they would not damage any of the nearby cars or houses. I found my baseball glove and just sat on my front lawn, watching the boys play. Our mailbox on the street was first base. I watched for a while and then retreated into my house—I was very shy. No more than five minutes passed and the doorbell rang. When my mother opened the door, she found all the boys had come to invite me to play too. I was so very happy in my new surroundings.

My new friends were mostly friendly. They would make fun of my New York accent, and we would occasionally debate the right way to pronounce a word or the proper use of a statement or brand name. For instance, I used to love vanilla malteds when I lived in the Bronx. Well, in Miami they were called shakes. A famous ice cream company that operates vendor trucks in New York is known as Mister Softee. My Miami friends insisted it was called Captain Softee. Even in school, the teachers pointed out how Northerners spoke differently than Floridians. One teacher wrote these words on the blackboard: "Merry, Mary, and Marry." As a former New Yorker, I was asked to pronounce the words as they were spelled. I responded: "Merry, Mary, Marry." My Floridian friends looked at the words on the blackboard and simply replied: "Mary, Mary, Mary."

In our elementary school music class, we were instructed to sing the song "Dixie" all together as a group. As a Yankee, I would never sing that song. While I hadn't yet learned the history of the South and the Confederacy, it just seemed wrong to be singing about the glory of the South and its culture when I identified with a different region of the country and its own culture. I still felt like a New Yorker.

The North and South also differed in their methods of disciplining students in the 1960s. In the Northern schools, your parents would be summoned for a parent-teacher conference. In the schools of South Florida, the principals used a wooden paddle to discipline an unruly student. A visit to the grocery store also had its own distinction. In the North, I found only one water fountain to drink from. In Miami, there were two water fountains in the back of the grocery stores, placed next to each other. Each water fountain had a small sign in front of it held by a chain link. The sign on the left read "Colored," while the sign on the right read "White."

The first time I saw this, I turned to my mother and,

pointing at the "Colored" sign, asked, "Will rainbow-colored water come out of that one?"

I had never experienced living in a segregated community and was not truly aware of what racism was yet. The issue of segregation did arise in my childhood years when our public school districts were redrawn for purposes of busing students to different schools to meet racial balance requirements of the federal government. I personally did not sense any discrimination in my neighborhood or schools in North Miami Beach as a result of my religion because the area was predominately Jewish when I was growing up.

In October 1962, my brother, Steven, paid an unannounced visit to South Florida. The United States was engaged in the Cuban Missile Crisis, and South Florida was in a war footing. Steven's army division, Old Ironsides, was transported from Fort Hood in Texas to Georgia, which was to serve as a staging area for US forces that were readied for an invasion of Cuba. Steven and his division departed in troop transport vessels and headed toward the island of Cuba, where they remained offshore, waiting for an order to begin the invasion.

In North Miami Beach, I saw military jeeps and vehicles heading down neighborhood streets and staging areas set up for military personnel on public school playgrounds. Fortunately, the crisis was ultimately averted and resolved, after which Steven's division returned to the States and docked in Port Everglades, just east of Fort Lauderdale. The division commander allowed Steven to come home for dinner with us before returning to his unit. We were so proud of Steven.

After his furlough and return to Fort Hood, his position as the jeep commander's driver had been given to someone else. Steven was upset and wanted out of the military. He made plans with a friend and ended up dishonorably discharged from the army for robbing a cigarette machine in the view of the military police, or MPs. They figured that was the best way out.

After this, he wound up back in South Florida, knocking on our door. My mother opened it and remarked, "Look what the wind blew in." She then abruptly closed the door in his face.

Steven never lived with us again and his relationship with our mother was severely strained for countless years. I wasn't allowed to see him since he had created many problems for himself and our family. But Steven was still my brother, and I loved him no differently. Claudia felt the same. If Steven was visiting town, she would tell our mother that we were going out to see a movie and we would visit him instead. When we were able to visit together, Steven asked me and Claudia how we were doing and about our schooling. He often expressed how much he missed us. He also let us know that he was managing fine on his own. It was always a warm and loving secretive time for us to spend together.

Claudia was five years older than me, and though we were somewhat close growing up, there was always a bit of tension between us. This was possibly caused by my behavior—I could nag my sister now and then. However, in hindsight, I believe it frustrated Claudia that I was loved and complimented by our parents because I was the "good kid" and hadn't done anything seriously wrong. It was a difficult moral standard, and she and Steven were always held up against it by our parents. I know that she loved and cared about me in her own way. In the Bronx, Claudia would sometimes take me to my Little League baseball games with her friend, Yvonne. Claudia and Yvonne were not so much interested in Little League, but they thought Stan, the baseball manager, was cute.

Claudia was a talented musician who played flute and piccolo masterfully. She became so good as a flutist that she auditioned for the High School of Music and Art in New York City and was accepted. It was a prestigious school of fine arts, and she had studied and practiced diligently for the opportunity. But then we relocated to Florida, and she was not able to attend. I am sure she felt dejected and very hurt when she could not pursue this academic opportunity she had earned.

She struggled to start over in Florida and had no friends in North Miami Beach, though she did have the occasional chance to visit with our cousins and relatives who lived nearby. Her social life primarily revolved around being a member of the Miami Norland High School Band as a flute player, and I followed in her footsteps a few years later, playing the saxophone. After graduating from high school, Claudia seemed to lose her path and passion.

Claudia attended the local community college for just two weeks. She had no career in mind, and I believe she was somewhat enticed by the lifestyle she could lead if living near our father in Las Vegas. Claudia dropped out of the community college and soon married her first husband, Dennis, whom she had just met the prior summer in upstate New York.

CHAPTER 5

A First Taste of Las Vegas

Growing up in North Miami Beach with my mother as a single parent was a stable environment for me. I learned and adhered to basic values and led an emotionally supportive and contented life at home. My weekdays were largely committed to school, band practice, and homework. At home, we played ball games on our street—stickball or baseball using a rubber ball, touch football, twenty-one, Indian Ball, and kickball. We also rode our bicycles often, attaching baseball cards to the wheelbase frame of the bike with clothespins so when the cards smacked against the spinning spokes of the wheel, it sounded like we were driving motorbikes. We had skateboards and roller skates too. Our after-school days of playing outside ended when our mothers yelled out to us from their kitchen windows that dinner was ready. It was a very nurturing and wonderful childhood, and I will always cherish it.

When I was thirteen years old, I took my first trip to Las Vegas to visit my father. My cousin Adrienne escorted me across the country, and we stayed at the Sands Hotel, where he worked. While I had traveled on planes before between New York and Miami, this was my first cross-country flight. We departed Miami on a National Airlines DC-8 jet aircraft, and the journey took over eight hours. There were not any nonstop flights operating between Miami and Las Vegas at the time, and we made intermediate stops in New Orleans and Houston, which added to the flight time.

Cross-country air travel was a wonderful new experience for me. I gazed out the window and marveled at the changes in landscapes from flat and green landmasses to crossing over the Mississippi River, to dramatic mountains with snow-capped peaks as we traveled over the Rockies.

The time in Las Vegas had been short in duration, and soon I was heading back, this time with Claudia escorting me. It was a surreal setting for a young teenager whose life in North Miami Beach mostly revolved around playing ball with his friends, listening to his shortwave radio, and practicing his alto saxophone.

While visiting Las Vegas had been a great experience, it was also confusing. Across the street from the Sands Hotel was the Castaways Hotel, with an adjoining souvenir shop. The store had a display sign that read: "Free Slot Machines That Really Work—Take One Home!" During my stay at the Sands, I walked across the street to see if I could get one of the free slot machines to take home. I was handed a small key chain with a plastic replica of a slot machine that had loose spinning reels inside. Well, I did take it home.

Las Vegas was a fantasy world, an adult Disneyland, and the words "normal" and "morality" were not commonly used to depict life in the hotel and gaming industry. This world comprised a mixture of people and interests, many of whom represented organized crime families from across the country. Of course, I didn't know any of that then. The executives who represented these interests and their spouses were mostly warm and friendly to me. As a teenager, I considered them as close family friends or pseudorelatives. Later, in my adult years, I learned more about them in the many books published about the influence of the Mob in Las Vegas.

This was an era when everything was high-class, and everyone was dressed up for the part. Suits and ties, dresses and gowns, and a respectful demeanor were expected by all. Business agreements in the gaming industry were sealed mostly with a handshake rather than a formal written contract. A breach of your agreement or promise with someone who was "connected" usually didn't result in court damages. The venue for resolving such disputes was the vast desert on the outskirts of the city. There was no judge or jury.

In the time before cell phones, guests were paged in a hotel if they received a phone call. "Telephone call for Mr. Cohen, Mr. Carl Cohen, please." Carl Cohen was an executive at the Sands Hotel and formerly from Cleveland. He was a tall and sturdy middle-aged man who was one of my father's bosses and mentors, as well as a close friend. He kept the peace among all the owners and associates of the Mob-owned hotels and casinos.

A story my father told me was about one morning while Carl was having his usual breakfast in the Garden Room of the Sands Hotel. During the prior evening, Frank Sinatra had been in the casino showing off his gambling talents at the tables. Surprisingly, Mr. Sinatra was told that evening his credit had been cut off as his casino debts ("markers") had become excessive. Mr. Sinatra was embarrassed and angered. He assumed that Carl had ordered his credit be cut off. So the next morning, Mr. Sinatra stormed into the Garden Room, spotted Carl seated, and, after approaching him, threw the dining table up and toward him while ranting and raving about what had happened.

Carl got up from his seat in his usual calm demeanor and

landed a swift punch to Mr. Sinatra's face, which dislodged some caps off Mr. Sinatra's front teeth. Sinatra threatened Carl, told him that his friends would take care of him, and left the Sands for the last time. My father shared with me that later in the day a message was delivered to Carl from the Desert Inn Hotel. The handwritten note stated, "Well done, Carl Cohen." It was signed by Howard Hughes, a famous industrialist and the owner of the Sands Hotel and other nearby hotel and casino establishments at the time. It was Mr. Hughes who had cut off Frank Sinatra's credit that prior evening. In the years that followed, whenever I would gain the praise of my father for an accomplishment, he would say to me, "Well done, Carl Cohen."

Carl Cohen was never retaliated against by the Mob interests for the appropriate actions he took against Mr. Sinatra. Many years later, Sinatra was asked about the incident. His response was "Never fight a Jew in the desert." It was very poignant that when Carl passed away many years later, his widow received flowers and a condolence card from Frank Sinatra.

Life at the Sands Hotel was like living in a movie. Because I was underage, I was only permitted to order fruit punches or soda in the hotel rooms and restaurants, while also being restricted from the casino. While my father worked evenings in the casino, I was escorted into the Copa Room to see so many of the great entertainers of the 1960s and '70s. I watched and enjoyed performances by Sammy Davis Jr., Steve Lawrence and Eydie Gormé, and the Carpenters. At other hotel properties I saw Johnny Carson, Don Rickles, Buddy Hackett, the Supremes, Ann-Margret, Rowan and Martin, Jerry Lewis, and even Andy Griffith and Lorne Greene, who attempted their own stage performances.

Lorne Greene was a lead actor in a popular television series called *Bonanza*. In the series, another actor, Michael Landon, played the part of one of the sons, named Little Joe.

When I attended Lorne Greene's show, I was seated in the front row. Greene reached out his hand to shake my hand and referred to me as "another Little Joe." I'm sure there were many more celebrities that I was fortunate to see in their Las Vegas shows. I was always treated so warmly and kindly because I was "Mickey's son."

When I was fourteen years old, I started traveling on my own to visit my father in Las Vegas during winter and summer vacations. The mental and emotional transition from a seemingly unhinged lifestyle in Las Vegas back to my stable existence in North Miami Beach was always a challenge. My energy was often depleted during these times, and it became a true emotional balancing act. But it was worth it because I sensed that my father wanted to spend more time with me and for both of us to get to know each other better and feel more comfortable together. As busy as his life was, I think he realized that the most significant time he had spent with me was before I turned four years old. I also wanted to develop a meaningful relationship with my father beyond the ten-minute phone calls we had most Sunday afternoons. We were still a mystery to each other.

Before the trips to Las Vegas, my father had made one previous effort to make sure I was not becoming a "mama's boy." He made plans for me to spend part of the summer on a supervised camping expedition with other children my age, known as Trails West. It was a mobile camp using five or six Volkswagen vans with attached tent structures that had to be assembled. Under the supervision of camp counselors, kids traveled to different national parks, sporting events, and other interesting places across the country over several weeks during the summer. While I would love to do that today, I refused to go and just didn't want to leave home at that time. So his initial attempt to toughen me up was unsuccessful.

Claudia and Dennis moved to Las Vegas with their new

son, Keith, in 1970. Having Claudia nearby when I would visit Las Vegas made my time with our father more comfortable and meaningful, as I missed her greatly. Dennis had no career training, so my father wanted to jump-start their married life and give them a path forward. He arranged for Dennis to attend a dealer's school in Las Vegas, and upon finishing his training, he became a card dealer downtown at the Fremont Hotel. For multiple reasons, the marriage was not a healthy one and did not last for more than another year. Claudia and Dennis divorced, and he left to pursue a life in California. Dennis had no future relationship with Claudia or his son; his parental rights to Keith were legally revoked as petitioned for by Claudia.

Ultimately, Claudia married twice, was involved in a third relationship, and had a total of three children. Claudia had been somewhat rebellious as a teenager, and she often conflicted with our mother, a rather strict parent who did not sugarcoat what she felt. Conversely, our father was more passive and complacent. I believe Claudia wasn't successful in her relationships because she placed our father so high up on a pedestal. She was enamored with his business life, his circle of interesting business associates, and the significant amount of money he was able to earn in his pursuits. It was a glamorous way to enjoy and experience life in Las Vegas, and she wanted to be a part of it. But none of her potential partners could compete with her love and affection for our father, which resulted in jealousy and dysfunction in her marriages and other serious relationships.

I was always amused by the strange nicknames that everyone in the Las Vegas community seemed to have. My father had a friend who owned a jewelry store known as T-Bird Jewels at the Thunderbird Hotel. His name was Mickey the Dude. There was a short man who was involved with the owners at Caesars Palace, Bobby the Midget. Due to his very short stature, he purportedly checked under the hotel owners' cars to make sure there were no explosive devices planted before they journeyed off the property. Uncle Nate had an old friend from New York who would visit Las Vegas now and then. Because the man had a flattened nose from his professional fighting career, his nickname was Flat-Nosed Moishe. A major junket operator from New York went by the name Big Louie. My father was affectionately referred to as Mickey Machine due to his love for and fascination with slot machines.

As my brother, Steve, had also moved to Las Vegas in the early 1970s, I spent time with him when I was visiting. On one memorable occasion together, Steve asked me to spend the day with him and his girlfriend at Lake Mead just outside Las Vegas. The plan was to cruise around the lake and view the desert scenery on the company boat, *Miss Bally*.

Steven lived life to the fullest and with an adventurous sense of humor. To me, spending the day on Lake Mead sounded like a pleasant and relaxing experience to simply enjoy. My brother had a different idea. Following our forty-five-minute drive through the intense summer heat of the Nevada desert, Steven, his girlfriend, and I arrived at the Callville Bay Marina. We brought our food and supplies onto the boat and then began our journey across the expansive lake. As I began to relax and enjoy the beautiful scenery of the deep blue water against the bordering beige desert landscape and jagged mountains, my brother thought he would make our journey more interesting and memorable. He encouraged his shapely girlfriend to sit at the bow of the boat while we continued across the lake, and she draped her large, exposed breasts over the railing, providing true shock value to passing boaters. This was a unique and unexpected experience for me. It was funny yet also very uncomfortable. I purposely did not make any eye contact with the oncoming boat passengers to see their reactions.

Steven would sometimes take me to the coffee shop of the Stardust Hotel to have vanilla shakes. On one occasion, he asked me if I had ever played keno. I told him I wasn't familiar—I was maybe sixteen years old at the time and under the legal age to participate in any gaming activities. He explained that you choose some numbers from a game display of eighty numbers, and if a certain number of the chosen numbers matched your selection, you won money. The keno cards, along with black marking crayons, were situated at each coffee shop booth, just as you would usually find a stack of napkins placed at a restaurant dining table.

"Glenn, take one of those blank keno cards and the black crayon and mark an X on any eight numbers on the card. After you mark up the card, a keno runner will come by the table, I will pay her $1.20 as the bet, and then she'll process the bet at the keno counter in the casino," Steven said.

I did so and the keno runner soon returned with a validated and stamped card indicating the wager placed for the next round of the game. Keno numbers were randomly displayed in the coffee shop and other locations in the casino. One by one, a number was illuminated on the board until twenty of the eighty possible numbers were selected. Steven told me that if at least five of my eight selected numbers lit up on the keno board, I could win $25.00.

The game began and I closely watched the numbers appearing on the board, comparing them to the numbers I had selected. Steven asked me how I was doing. I was checking each of the numbers being drawn and displayed on the lighted game panel on the coffee shop wall.

"Steve! I have five numbers!" I exclaimed.

"Great, you won twenty-five bucks!" said Steve.

"I have six numbers—wait, now I have seven!"

"Let me see your card!" he said. He took my winning keno

card and ran out of the coffee shop to collect the winnings. When he came back to our table, he showed me the cash, fanning it out like playing cards in a spread. He was holding $2,200! He was so excited. Steve handed me $300 and told me that he needed to keep the rest for paying taxes on the winnings. He also gave the keno runner a $100 tip, and she spent that evening with him.

I saw my father that evening and shared the good news of my win with him. My father stared at me and for the first and probably only time in my life, he reprimanded me. He told me that I should never gamble, especially if I ever wanted to be successful in the gaming industry or in life. He was adamant about it. He had witnessed too many businesspeople become addicted to gambling and turn down a depressing road that ruined life for themselves and their families. I listened to his advice, and since that time, the extent of my personal wagering is twenty dollars in a draw poker machine maybe once a year.

Today, as a gaming law attorney and adjunct professor, I counsel my clients and instruct my students on the dire impact of compulsive gambling for an individual and their families, leading to mental health issues, financial insecurity, and, in some cases, much worse. Recalling my father's conversation about gambling and later witnessing the consequences of a gambling addiction in someone close to me have always kept me in line.

At the office, my father was occasionally visited by women who wanted to be introduced to hotel entertainment managers on the Las Vegas Strip for an opportunity to be cast in a hotel show production. They knew that my father had business relationships with hotel and casino owners and that a recommendation could be made by him for an audition with their entertainment managers. These women performed some unique show talent for my father so that an appropriate introduction could be made. The stories I heard about their auditions were generally adult-rated, reaffirming my impression of Las Vegas being an adult Disneyland.

There were many meals out with businesspeople, friends, and family members of which I have very fond recollections. My father always enjoyed a fine Italian dinner, and I would hear stories about his love for pasta. He had a favorite restaurant in Milan, Italy, where he purportedly ordered pasta as his main course and more pasta for dessert. In Las Vegas, some of the memorable Italian restaurants we visited in the 1960s and '70s included Bombaro's, which was near the base of Sunrise Mountain; Larry's Restaurant and Cioppino's, both on East Charleston Boulevard; and Gourmet Corner and the Venetian Ristorante on Sahara. Each restaurant has its own special memory for me.

Bombaro's was a small, family-owned Italian restaurant featuring a sign above the dining room entryway that said: "If you don't like garlic, go home." What was peculiar about Bombaro's was that they had a strict reservation policy. Even if their restaurant was totally empty of customers, they still would not seat you without a reservation.

Larry's Restaurant was owned by an Italian gentleman named—you guessed it—Larry, whose specialties included a wonderful linguine and clam sauce. Larry claimed that he personally prepared shipments of his pasta sauce to send to Lucky Luciano, who had been deported to Sicily.

Cioppino's was a fine Italian restaurant that featured its daily menu exclusively on a blackboard. While the Italian meals were wonderful there, the business closed due to the owner's crippling gambling addiction. It was the usual pattern. A business owner begins to gamble excessively and uncontrollably. They then use all the company profits to support the habit, are unable to address their business supplies and overhead, approach their good customers for personal loans, and it goes downhill from there.

The Gourmet Corner was owned by a wonderful couple, Peggy and Piero. Piero gained a very strong following for his culinary skills and his name later graced restaurants where he was the chef. He created such wonderful culinary masterpieces that celebrities sought him out. My father told me that one night the Gourmet Corner was packed with customers when Piero and Peggy received a call that Frank Sinatra and his entourage were coming to dinner. Piero purportedly announced to everyone that they all needed to leave because "Frank is coming!" I always noticed the picture of Piero and Frank Sinatra, which was proudly displayed on the counter of all Piero's restaurants.

The Venetian Ristorante was also a fine Italian restaurant that catered to families and offered takeout. I went to the Venetian for lunch or dinner many times, even in my adult years.

Breakfast or lunch was usually at Poppa Gar's Restaurant, which was off Western Avenue. It was a small place where locals went and one of the power broker locations visited by politicians of the day. Poppa Gar was a tall and unassuming man in his early senior years. All the usual breakfast and lunch items were offered, but it was the decor that I found challenging. In addition to framed pictures of many of his favorite guests, there were at least fifteen wall-mounted animal heads, from bighorn sheep to deer. Poppa Gar was an avid hunter and proudly exhibited the taxidermized evidence of his conquests, but for a boy who grew up in a suburban East Coast Jewish neighborhood, it was quite the sight.

My father placed two or three slot machines in Poppa Gar's Restaurant as part of his gaming route. The games didn't realize much in revenues as restaurants were not known to be prime slot route locations, but my father had a good relationship with Poppa Gar. I recall one day after we left lunch at Poppa Gar's and were returning to his office, my father exclaimed, "Oh my God, I forgot to pay the bill. Poppa Gar is going to throw a stroke!" We immediately returned and paid the bill. Poppa Gar was just fine.

On Sunday mornings, I found most of the Jewish hotel operatives having breakfast at Jackie's Deli, which was in the back section of White Cross Drugs in Commercial Center. It was a weekly ritual followed by the hotel and casino business personalities for many years.

My father had a favorite story about a restaurant he once frequented in Los Angeles that served some very rich and heavy entrées. He would be there, having a fine dinner until the server interrupted the patrons by placing a placard on the table that read "Intermission." All the diners were then escorted into a garden area, where there was an old-fashioned weight-reducing machine. The dining patrons took turns with the weight-reducing belt, which, when placed around the midsection, would shake the belly back and forth. Purportedly, this movement compacted the already ingested food to allow the diners to enjoy the next course. Whether or not this was true, my father always liked reciting the story.

There is a reason why I have gone into so much detail about the restaurants of the early times in Las Vegas. My father was not a golfer or a sports enthusiast. He believed that food offered the best way to pursue business opportunities, and many important transactions took place over lunch or a fine dining experience. In fact, I once asked my father why he traveled first-class on planes when it was so expensive compared to other booking options. He simply replied, "Who am I going to discuss business with in coach?"

The owners of the Sands Hotel were not only a cast of business executives but at times a kind of brotherhood who would protect each other and their interests, even if those interests weren't so savory. My father once shared with me that one of the Rat Pack entertainers had transgressed with an underage woman. The hotel owners needed to deal with it privately before it became a very concerning public relations matter. The resolution of this sensitive situation entailed the aggrieved party accepting a cash settlement in addition to her parents signing a nondisclosure agreement.

On another evening, the owners had to handle a very delicate matter. One of the hotel owners received a frantic late-night call—it was his business partner's mistress. She was extremely upset and needed immediate help as the business partner had just suffered a heart attack and died while they were romantically engaged. The problem? His wife was asleep in their residence upstairs in the same building. They needed to consider what to do. The hotel owners and my father banded together and quickly arrived at the scene. They confirmed that their friend had expired and carried his body back to his own residence. My father was given the key, but he was so nervous that his hands were shaking and he just couldn't fit the key into the lock. Eventually, someone managed to open the door, and they quietly placed the body somewhere in the residence—all while his wife was fast asleep in the bedroom. Then they all left.

The next morning when the wife awoke to find her husband dead, she called the sheriff's office and the rest of the hotel owners, who quickly came to support her. The body was examined, the sheriff looked around the room at everyone, and then he simply concluded, probably with a wink, that this individual had passed away at home peacefully in his sleep. These stories always shocked me, and the impression I had of the shady business life and workings in Las Vegas grew with each new event I learned about.

Following each new episode of Las Vegas intrigue, I

returned home to North Miami Beach and it would take a couple of weeks before I could enjoy playing ball with my friends on the street, practicing my alto saxophone for band practice and concerts, and listening to late-night shortwave radio shows on my radio set again.

My father also visited me in South Florida a few times a year. Sometime during the mid-1960s, he took me with him to the presentation of a new jukebox product at the Dupont Plaza Hotel in downtown Miami. The jukebox was a Scopitone, the first attempt to produce music videos. It was a somewhat primitive music video device that had a small screen at the top of the machine that would show a video of go-go dancers moving to the music; though, in the version I saw, there was no coordination between the selected song and how the dancers performed. The presentation was well attended by connected movers and shakers, and the product was heavily invested in. But it failed to make a significant impact in the entertainment market for various reasons. The Scopitone was novel, but it needed refinement. In addition, once it became public knowledge that the majority of shareholders behind the product were reputed members of organized crime, the marketability of the product was tainted.

On his visits, my father and I went to a game arcade on the Seventy-Ninth Street Causeway in Miami known as Fun Fair. I enjoyed playing the pinball machines and having a hot dog and soda, while my father engaged in conversation with the owner. We also traveled to Miami Beach to visit Uncle Nate, who spent the winters at the Governor Hotel near Twenty-First Street. We'd meet Uncle Nate at a luncheonette stand on the north side of the Seagull Hotel, a business that was owned and operated by some family friends from the Catskills. My uncle spent most of his time there. It was an odd setting since Twenty-First Street and Collins Avenue was the site of one of the first openly gay beaches in Miami during the 1960s. Uncle

Nate was not gay, but I believe the setting added camouflage to his real reason for hanging out there.

I learned years later that Uncle Nate not only managed the family bakery in Hurleyville but was also employed as a bookmaker for the S&G Syndicate, controlled by mobster Meyer Lansky. Uncle Nate would accept bets from those placing wagers at the luncheonette stand or by phone from out-of-state wagerers, then drive to Hialeah Park Race Track to place the bets. The luncheonette owner's son was a member of the Miami Beach Police Department. The location was raided on several occasions, but the raids were more staged and ceremonial than any real enforcement of gambling laws. It was all to give the appearance of law and order being maintained. If there were any arrests, they were for public appearance only, and the arrestees were quietly and promptly released.

When I was a teenager, my father occasionally asked me to drive him from North Miami Beach up to Boca Raton to visit his friends, Abe and Harriet Green. He had met Abe Green through Uncle Nate when he was a teenager. We would drive up on a weekend day and find our way to the Boca Teeca Country Club. I had met Abe Green on a couple of occasions in New Jersey when my father took me to his amusement machine business known as Runyon Sales. I didn't know much about Abe Green at the time, and he seemed to be a good family man, a very tall and handsome individual who was well dressed and exhibited a strong and self-assured demeanor. When we visited, my father privately chatted with Abe in his screened-in terrace overlooking the golf course. They talked together for maybe thirty minutes, while I sat on the living room sofa and his wife, Harriet, offered me something.

"Glenn, please don't get involved in this when you grow up," Harriet said to me on one visit, weariness clear in her voice.

"I won't," I told her, but I had no clue what she was talking about. We concluded our visits by having dinner together in the Boca Teeca Clubhouse Restaurant, and then we'd head back to Miami, where I'd drop my father off at his hotel.

When I got married in 1976 in downtown Miami, one of the invited guests was Abe Green. After the wedding, my father pulled me aside and requested that any photographs of Abe be removed and disposed of from the proofs, and I did it without asking any questions. Years later, my sister-in-law Sherry shared that on that day, she and her husband, Robert, decided to take a break from the wedding reception. They went out to the parking lot for a few minutes of fresh air and saw two men in dark suits walking from car to car, writing down license plate numbers. As Sherry was never a shy person, she approached these two gentlemen and asked, "What do you think you're doing?" The stern response she received was: "Mind your business, young lady." The individuals were either Nevada Gaming Control Board enforcement agents or, more likely, FBI agents.

My understanding is that Abe was involved in some early criminal activities in New Jersey in the 1930s, which included hijacking shipments of valuable merchandise, such as furs and government-confiscated alcohol. When law enforcement was after Abe, Uncle Nate hid him and his associates in the upstairs bedrooms of Wichinsky's Bake Shop or at nearby farms owned by mutual friends until the heat was off. Years later, Abe became the front man for the ownership of Bally Manufacturing. The individual he was fronting was Gerardo (Jerry) Catena, the underboss of the Vito Genovese crime family of New Jersey. Gerardo Catena also held a silent ownership interest in the Sands Hotel and Casino in Las Vegas during the early 1950s and '60s, along with his partner, Meyer Lansky. And the connections didn't stop there. My cousin Robert, Aunt Pauline's son, was once married to Geraldine Catena, the daughter of underboss Gerardo Catena.

When my father was first forming a relationship with Abe, Abe asked my father to drive him from New Jersey to Baltimore for a business meeting. My father drove him there and back on the same day, and they had no discussions during the full day's journey. When they arrived back in Springfield at Abe's office, Abe thanked my father and remarked: "You know what I like about you, Mickey? You don't say anything."

CHAPTER 6

Bally Comes to Nevada

Sometime during the mid- to late 1960s, my father was granted the distribution rights to sell Bally slot machines in southern Nevada. Bally Manufacturing was based in Chicago, and it was expanding its gaming machine market and footprint worldwide. My father opened his Bally distributorship in Las Vegas and formed Bally Sales Corporation of Nevada. Bally Manufacturing had set up two distributorships for its sales and marketing efforts in Nevada, with a second distributorship granted to a gaming and amusement industry veteran from Mississippi. That man, Si Redd, opened his Bally distribution company in Reno for the northern Nevada market and formed Bally Distributing Company. By formal agreement, Si was permitted to market Bally slot machines in Nevada anywhere north of an imaginary line that ran west to east from the town of Tonopah, Nevada, and my father could market the machines anywhere south of the line.

Bally slot machines became the premier gaming machine in the slot industry. Bally had created the first electromechanical slot machine, replacing the older mechanical slot machines manufactured by companies like Mills and Jennings. Bally had its initial difficulties with its new slot machine, known as the Money Honey, but with the technical and mechanical assistance that my father and other individuals working with Bally provided, the Money Honey became a worldwide success. The electromechanical slot machine had many visual and play functions that far exceeded what a mechanical slot machine could offer a player or casino. My father discovered the hopper unit and introduced it to Bally, which significantly enhanced the operation of the slot machine. The hopper was a rotating metal bin located in the slot machine where inserted coins would be stored for possible electronic payouts to the customer. If the hopper became full of coins, the excess coins would fall into the drop bucket, located below in the slot stand. This resulted in the casino profits earned by that particular slot machine. Bally slot machines incorporating the new hopper could track and pay out large coin jackpots of thousands of coins, whereas the older mechanical slot machines were mostly limited to a twenty-coin payout.

Between my father's hotel ownership and management relationships and Steven's assistance, Bally Sales Corporation easily sold these new electromechanical slot machines to Las Vegas Strip hotel locations in lots of eight hundred units or more per sale. Bally gained much of the market share for slot machines in the worldwide gaming industry. Singer Dean Martin accompanied Abe Green, then president of Bally Manufacturing, to persuade hotel and casino owners on the Strip to purchase the new Bally slots, which greatly boosted sales. I have been told that Dean Martin and Abe later became close friends.

Bally Sales Corporation had many years of success until around 1971, when three incidents worked against my father. Si Redd, who later founded the international giant gaming company International Game Technology (IGT), decided to be more aggressive in his sales tactics. He began to disregard the established territories for the two Bally distributorships. Si purportedly sold directly into the Las Vegas market, which was supposed to be a protected territory for my father. Si offered my father's existing customers a dollar per day per machine to remove my father's Bally slot machines and replace them with his own Bally slot machine of the same or similar models. This financial arrangement would continue so long as the Bally games placed by Si remained in operation on the casino floor.

This tactic did not increase overall sales or placements of Bally slot machines in Nevada; it primarily benefited Si Redd in his positioning for expanded Bally distribution rights in Nevada. While this was very upsetting to my father, apparently, Bally Manufacturing was pleased with Si's aggressive marketing style, which proved very effective in Bally gaining the majority of the market share for slot machines in Nevada.

It was also around this same time that my father's company, Bally Sales Corporation, was under scrutiny by the State of Nevada Gaming Control Board. The regulatory authority could revoke gaming licenses if they discovered that an individual or a company had associations with disreputable people in business or in life, including those with criminal and unsavory backgrounds. This was why Mob bosses were not openly in charge of gaming businesses. Instead, they had fronts, or people with clean backgrounds, to run the company for them. While Abe Green was president of Bally Manufacturing, one of his silent investors was Gerardo Catena. While Si Redd probably had similar dealings with the Bally Manufacturing organization in Chicago, it was my father who was targeted and investigated by the Gaming Control Board.

In 1971, I was attending the University of Miami as a sophomore, enjoying college life and totally unaware of the dire situation my father was facing. Twenty-five hundred miles away in Las Vegas, a raid was conducted on Bally Sales Corporation by agents of the Nevada Gaming Control Board. My father was charged with having business associations with criminal or unsavory individuals and was brought forward for a public hearing to adjudge him. My father risked the loss of his business, his career, and his ability to provide for his family should the Gaming Control Board rule against him.

My father retained the best legal counsel, as he was represented by the law firm of the former governor of Nevada, Grant Sawyer. The findings in the hearing indicated that my father had indeed associated with unsavory individuals as prohibited under the gaming laws of the State of Nevada. He ultimately received a formal reprimand for his conduct from the Gaming Control Board but was permitted to maintain his gaming license in good standing.

Possibly as a result of additional government intimidation against my father (and Bally Manufacturing), a grand jury was convened at this time to determine whether my father should be prosecuted for tax evasion. Archived newspaper articles refer to a jury trial held in federal court in southern Nevada on the charges brought against my father. The trial lasted for one week, and the jury acquitted my father on all charges.

Once the hearings were finalized and the court proceedings were dismissed against my father, those in power at Bally Manufacturing decided that it was time for my father's distributorship to be acquired and for my father to leave the company. Bally Sales Corporation of Nevada was sold to Si Redd's company, Bally Distributing Company, for approximately $650,000. My father identified himself with Bally and his business colleagues for so many of his early years that I have to assume this was a personally hurtful experience for him at that stage of his life.

In 1972, now totally free to conduct himself independently

in the gaming industry, my father had a plan to create his own slot machines and gaming devices. He established his own company, Games of Nevada, and purchased some unimproved real estate that had an abandoned gas station on the lot. He removed the gas station structure and large gas storage tanks underground before designing and constructing his 14,500-square-foot factory and office facility. This was the headquarters for Games of Nevada, located at 2575 South Highland Drive in Las Vegas.

I still had no knowledge of what had transpired at Bally. I was busy pledging to join a fraternity, practicing halftime show routines with the University of Miami Band of the Hour, dating, and generally enjoying the college social life.

I spent the summers of 1972 and '73 visiting my father and his second wife, Zola. I met Zola when I was thirteen years old. She was a very attractive and tall woman with long blond hair, and I first saw her in the hallway of the Raleigh Hotel in South Fallsburg, New York, where my bar mitzvah reception was being held. Zola had accompanied my father on the trip, but she was not an invited guest since no one knew about her at the time. They met in Las Vegas when Zola was working at the Riviera Hotel. She had been a dancer and later a cocktail server in the casino.

Once my father became an executive at the Sands, he asked Zola to leave her job as a cocktail server at the Riviera and move over to the Sands in the same capacity. While most of the female cocktail servers wore their skirts above their knees, my father made sure that Zola's were longer. He was possessive and probably had a jealous streak as well. I remember him joking with Zola about how she once had a close relationship with a gentleman whose nickname was Ice Pick Willie—I'd later learn he was a criminal known to kill his victims with an ice pick.

After the Sands was sold, Zola became a dedicated house-wife. They lived in an old ranch-style home on Lacy Lane on the west side of town. She had a deep heart for my father, his children, and her own. She hadn't attended much formal schooling but was self-made, engaging in home improvement projects—even doing her own construction. She didn't like to travel or go out to dinner meetings with my father. I truly cared about Zola and enjoyed spending time with her when I visited.

My father was good to us children, but he was not so wonderful to his wives. He often lived a double life when it came to romantic relationships, and these transgressions were always challenging for me to accept. I was respectful to his partners, but I did not want anyone to assume that I condoned his actions or that I was a son who didn't fall far from the tree.

While Zola was kind and caring to my father at home, he apparently felt he needed more in his life without letting go of what he had at home. He wanted a foundational marriage at home for emotional security but also needed to have someone in his life who would be willing to travel with him on business trips. He missed the company of someone who had greater business acumen and aspirations than his wife. He found this person in Connie Koplow.

He was introduced to Connie by a friend, and she became his other life partner for the ensuing thirty years. Connie was a ceramics and art professor at the local community college, a very intelligent woman for whom my father had deep affection. Connie worked as my father's assistant for many years, which Zola was aware of. However, any concerns Zola may have had about Connie were tempered by the fact that Claudia implied to Zola that Connie was gay. Claudia, always protective of our father, expressed this to Zola of her own volition in order to cover for my father's activities and social transgressions. Of course, it was not true. In later years, Zola became aware of the true nature of their relationship.

It was during this period in the early 1970s that Claudia married her second husband, David, an amateur boxer who was an old high school friend of Steven's. They had a daughter together, but their hopeful marriage was challenged by Claudia's overriding devotion to our father and David's addiction to drugs.

I really liked David, and he became a brother figure to me. He taught me about fine clothing, French suits and labels, how sports jackets should be properly fitted to your shoulders, and how your dress slacks should break correctly on top of your shoes. He also taught me to keep a crowbar under the front seat of my car for protection. David was not very tall, but he was muscular and would often walk around without a shirt, even while shopping. He used a personal sunlamp and kept pancake makeup with him to cover his slightly pitted complexion. He had been the Golden Gloves champion for his weight class in New York City, and his trainer was famed welter/middleweight boxer Emile Griffith. While David was always warm and caring to me, I believe he was jealous of the lack of attention he received from Claudia. Maybe overly jealous.

During their brief marriage, Claudia had a German shepherd named Shawn. Shawn was like a child to Claudia, and she lavished her love and attention on him. One day, Shawn went missing and was never found. There were suspicious blood spots in the bathtub, though, and the assumption was that David became so jealous of Claudia's attention to her dog that he killed Shawn and disposed of him in the desert. Shortly thereafter, Claudia and David separated.

One morning, while I was staying at my father and Zola's home on Lacy Lane, there was a knock on my bedroom door. I opened the door to see two police officers.

"Did you hear any gunshots early this morning, son?" one of them asked.

"No," I responded, my heart beating quickly. My bedroom was at the back of the house, and I had not heard anything.

"Come with us."

I got up and walked to the front bedroom of the house, where more police were examining damage to the windows and structure. The officers were talking to my father, who said, "Yes, I heard some noise early this morning, but it didn't sound like gunshots, and I wasn't concerned."

There was a witness, though. A young boy on his paper route saw a man stop his car in front of the house, roll down a window, and begin emptying a gun into my father and Zola's home. The paperboy noted the description of the car, a beige-and-white Cadillac Eldorado, and the license plate number. Later that morning, the police arrested David and his new girlfriend and found the weapon in a locker at the downtown Las Vegas bus station. David was an intense person who was easily emotionally triggered, and he was furious at Claudia about their split. My father didn't press charges, but private side arrangements were made so that David could never return to Nevada. Always on high alert for illegal activity surrounding gaming licensees, the Gaming Control Board began an investigation into the incident. But besides being front-page news, the matter soon faded away. After that, my father and Zola named the front bedroom riddled with bullet holes the Bugsy Siegel Room.

Sometime in the mid-1970s, there was another serious incident that I've only been able to piece together over years of accumulating bits of information. It related to a Mob effort to muscle in on my father's slot machine manufacturing and route business in Las Vegas. Claudia was a client of a popular hairstylist in Las Vegas who also catered to the entertainment industry; I'll call him Eddie. Eddie also had Mob connections. I assume that my sister may have shared some information about our father and the family business with Eddie during one of her many hairstyling appointments with him. This apparently piqued his interest.

Allegedly, Eddie shared his information about our family gaming business with associates of the Detroit Mob family. They made an effort to muscle into my father's business and gain a financial foothold in it. My father felt that if he did not accede to their demands, his life and family would be in immediate danger. The situation intensified when Claudia was attacked in the backyard of her home—an unknown assailant struck her in the back of the head with a blunt instrument. I would only learn after my father's passing how deeply my father feared for all our lives. He began taking lessons on how to shoot a handgun.

Abe Green, my father's trusted mentor, would occasionally call the office, but saying his name aloud in the office would cause concern for my father. Once, when I was in the office and Abe Green called, I simply told my father it was "Mr. Lincoln." This way, his announced identification as a caller would not be a dramatic moment. I dubbed him this because his first name was Abe, just like the sixteenth president. The nickname stuck, and that's what we said whenever he called. My father was also concerned about wiretaps and listening devices at the time, probably a result of having had his office telephones previously wiretapped by law enforcement prior to the raid of his offices at Bally Sales Corporation.

My father made some phone calls to Mr. Lincoln about the serious problem he was facing with the Detroit Mob–connected individuals. My father could not fight them on his own, so he hoped to use the power of his past connections to push them back and keep them away from his family.

Abe contacted Jerry Catena about the problem, though he

had retired from Mob activities by that time and was living peacefully in Boca Raton. Not only was Mr. Catena the former underboss of the Vito Genovese family, but he was also the former father-in-law of my cousin Robert, so he agreed to briefly step out of retirement to assist my father.

Mr. Catena purportedly placed a telephone call to the Florida Mob boss in Tampa, reputed to be Santo Trafficante. He was advised as to what my father was dealing with in Las Vegas. Mr. Catena asked him to call the head of the Detroit Mob family to have them step back from any pressuring efforts of associates trying to move into my father's business. This series of phone calls apparently made the difference in my father's life, and after that last one, my father was never pressured by the Mob or Mob forces again.

In contrast to my father's life-and-death issues, my life was sheltered. I lived a very normal, middle-class existence in North Miami Beach during my teenage years and into my early twenties. I had originally planned to study meteorology and become a weather forecaster. While attending the University of Miami, I also worked as an intern at the National Hurricane Center, which was on the top floor of the science building on campus. I was involved with the experts reviewing color-enhanced satellite imagery to determine how hurricanes would develop in strength and in what direction they might be steered by air currents and other atmospheric conditions. I even volunteered to assist in a federal government program known as SKYWARN, which was a network of local and regional spotters who reported any threatening weather patterns or developing tornados in the interest of public safety.

Being a meteorologist was a dream that began in childhood when my mother bought me a children's book I read often, *Weather and Climate*. However, by the time I began undergraduate studies in my late teens, the best education and training at the time for becoming a meteorologist was in the

US Navy. But the Vietnam War was still ongoing, and I was not planning to enlist. In addition, a meteorologist's annual salary in the mid-1970s was not much more than $30,000. My father said to me at the time: "If you are not making at least $100,000 a year, you are wasting your time." I then began to question my own thinking and career options.

My father and mother independently concurred that my future would be most promising and rewarding if I joined the family business in Las Vegas. Although becoming a meteorologist was my hope and dream, I didn't receive the emotional support to pursue this career path from either of my parents, and their opinions were very important to me at that stage of my life. I always wanted to please my parents.

So, although personally disappointed, I ultimately changed my college major to political science, volunteered for the presidential campaign of New York Mayor John Lindsay, and became a delegate to the 1972 Democratic National Convention at the age of eighteen. It was my first entry into the world of politics; I would later run for public office.

CHAPTER 7

Overseas Business Travel

Before I decided to join the family business, during college vacations, I traveled with my father on his trips. We visited his business friends and colleagues in New York, Chicago, New Orleans, and Los Angeles. He also invited me on some of his international trips, including my first overseas travel to St. Maarten and Antigua in the Caribbean, Hong Kong, Taipei, and Japan. I also got the chance to work with him at the international gaming exposition held in London.

Traveling with my father internationally was an adventure. We met such interesting people and dined in the finest restaurants, and he always made sightseeing plans for me while he was busy with his business meetings.

Once while at the airport he told me, "If I am ever delayed entering a country or reentering the US, just go ahead and get transportation to where we are staying, okay, Glenn?"

"Why would you be delayed at customs on a business trip?" I asked.

"Well, there is another Michael Wichinsky, a Canadian

national born on the same month, day, and year as me," my father replied. Apparently, this other Michael Wichinsky was engaged in some questionable activities and was on a government watch list. My father was always very persuasive, and it was a good story that I believed without question for many years.

When we visited Asia together in 1971, we first stopped in Hong Kong and checked into the presidential suite of the Hyatt Hotel located on the Kowloon Peninsula. My father's gaming industry friends—George D'Arcy of the Sands Hotel; Ray Torin, a gaming business operator from London; and Bill Capri, a Las Vegas hotel operative who had many ties in the worldwide-connected gaming industry—visited us in the hotel suite.

I was to take a tour around Hong Kong, the New Territories, and Victoria on Hong Kong Island with Ray's wife while my father's business friends and colleagues talked shop. To meet Mrs. Torin, I walked to the Star Ferry terminal in Kowloon and journeyed across Hong Kong harbor. In a totally foreign setting, it was surreal walking among crowds of people, pushing and shoving my way through the crowded ferry terminal with signs that read: "Spitting is prohibited." I met up with Mrs. Torin on Hong Kong Island, and we visited Victoria, the Jumbo Floating Restaurant, and Victoria Peak, later enjoying four o'clock tea in a very British hotel in this former colony of the United Kingdom.

One day, my father was excited about traveling to an address on Hong Kong Island, No. 1 Repulse Bay. This was the residential address of the late Asian gaming industry magnate Stanley Ho. As a result of his meetings with Stanley Ho, my father soon installed the first Bally electromechanical slot machines on the casino floor of Mr. Ho's prime hotel and casino property in Macau, the Hotel Lisboa.

From Hong Kong, we traveled to Taipei, where we met

with officials from the US military for placement of the new Bally slot machines at the officers' clubs operating at US military bases on the island of Taiwan. Currently, three branches of the US military permit gaming machines at the officers' clubs on foreign military bases.

Relations between Taiwan and Mainland China were extremely tenuous in the 1970s. Upon final approach to Taipei airport in the evening, the runway lights were unlit until the incoming aircraft's identity was recognized and confirmed. There were even manned machine gun posts placed in between the operating runways as a result of the tense relations.

While I was in Taiwan, I visited the National Museum of History, which contained rare and historic artifacts from China that were brought to Taiwan by the escaping Nationalist government in 1949, during the Chinese Revolution. It was an amazing collection.

Our final stop on our transpacific journey brought us to Tokyo. We met with my father's close friend Mike Kogan, who was the founder of the Taito Trading Company and creator of the very successful video game *Space Invaders*. I toured Tokyo with Mike Kogan's daughter, Rita. We visited the Tokyo Tower and the grounds of the Imperial Palace, then went to a nightclub known as Byblos with her boyfriend. My father, meanwhile, was involved in his business meetings. He always stayed at the Hotel Okura in Tokyo, and many years later when I traveled to Japan with my own children, we stayed at the Hotel Okura to continue the family tradition.

One evening in Tokyo with my father, we went to what I believe was the Copacabana, a famous private club owned and operated by a very strong-willed businesswoman known as Mama Cherry. This was a place visited by the personalities of the Rat Pack era, which included noted politicians, power brokers, and entertainers. Celebrities gathered there for food, drink, entertainment, and other pleasurable adult activities.

I was escorted into a large room in this establishment with eight to ten chairs set up in a large semicircle. We all sat down—my father, the businessmen in his party, and me. Then, young Japanese women in short skirts entered the room and sat down on each person's lap. I was puzzled and also quite naive at the time. The young woman sitting on me quietly shared that the other women were softly giggling at me.

"Why?" I asked.

"You don't know what's going on here, do you?"

"Of course I do," I said quickly. I didn't.

Apparently, the club offered private and intimate personal services to its patrons. I quickly excused myself and the evening ended, for me at least, as innocently and uneventfully as it began. I assume my father wanted me to experience another one of life's adult passions, but I just wasn't interested.

The next day, I was in the lobby of the Hotel Okura with Jed, the son of my father's dear friend David (Gabe) Forman. Jed and I learned that we had two things in common: Our fathers were in the same business and working with the same people, and we both loved the New York Yankees. Jed showed me his bent thumb. He had attended a Yankee baseball camp with some of the noted veteran players of the team. One day while catching, Jed broke his thumb. It was such a special moment for him with the Yankees that he never got his thumb set to heal properly. He was a true Yankees fan!

Jed introduced me to an acquaintance called Junko, a Japanese woman. After we all spoke together for some time about Tokyo and Japanese culture, Junko said she had to leave. She wrote down her name and phone number, along with her hours of availability, on a napkin and gave it to me. I was so innocent.

The last overseas trip my father and I took together was in 1975 from Miami to London to attend the annual gaming exposition, which I still go to every year. On our way to the Miami International Airport, we stopped at the famous Pumpernik's restaurant in Miami Beach to pick up some deli sandwiches for the overnight transatlantic flight. On the plane, most passengers were asleep when we opened our corned beef and pastrami sandwiches. I could see the noses of some passengers begin to twitch as the aroma of Jewish deli sandwiches pervaded the entire cabin.

We arrived in London and checked into our hotel room at the London Hilton on Park Lane in Mayfair. My father had made some advance plans for me to have a good time while visiting London by setting me up on a social date with Elaine, the daughter of one of his London gaming business colleagues.

One evening, Elaine and I went out with her brother and his girlfriend. It was fun to attend the opening of a new play in Chelsea called *The Rocky Horror Picture Show*, which later became a cult movie. Following the play, we had dinner at a new rock music–themed restaurant called the Hard Rock Cafe. The London location was the first of this now-worldwide brand. Being fixed up on a date by my father was a new experience for me, but it was also my first chance to experience the social life of a city in another country with others of my own age. I really enjoyed this night out in London.

I was always proud of my father's inventive mind as it related to new games and gaming technology, his wealth of friends around the world, and how he could incorporate his work, friendships, and worldwide travel in such an enriching and enjoyable lifestyle. I never believed that I would follow in his footsteps and enjoy exploring so many places in the world as an integral part of my own life and career.

CHAPTER 8

Games of Nevada

When I returned home to Florida from these exciting overseas trips with my father, I always looked forward to seeing my mother; my dog, Peanuts; and my girlfriend, Lillie.

I met Lillie in the eighth grade at John F. Kennedy Junior High School in North Miami Beach. We were both members of the school band. I played alto saxophone, and she played the clarinet. My first recollection of Lillie was when she was the band secretary and would hand out sheet music to all the musicians.

Once we were members of the high school marching band, I began to take closer note of her. One of the highlights of being a member of the marching band was going on out-of-town trips to perform halftime shows during football games. In my junior year, we were informed that we would be performing a halftime show somewhere in the Ocala/Orlando vicinity. As the bus rides to these out-of-town games were long, it was customary for band members to ask each other to sit with them. It was kind of a date, with an opportunity to converse and get to know each other better.

I was planning to approach Lillie and ask her to sit with me on the band bus for this trip, but I found out that my fellow saxophone player, Billy, had asked three girls to accompany him. One of them was Lillie. I approached Billy and expressed how unfair that was, so he asked Lillie to sit with me. Lillie was pretty, friendly, and giddy with big brown eyes and long brown hair pulled back in a ponytail. We took our first band trip seated next to each other. We stopped at a game farm where deer walked freely around the compound, and one of the deer began to munch on the hem of Lillie's white button-down sweater.

We started dating after that, but she had to follow the rules laid down by her parents: She could only go out on a double date, and she had an 11:00 p.m. curfew. Going out on a date without a car was difficult enough, but to arrange a double date and get her home before curfew made it more of a challenge. My best friend, Bob Levy, was open to being set up on a date with Lillie's friend Tourea, and he got permission from his mother to use her car. So our first date was to see a movie all together at the old Hollywood Mall. The movie was *The Impossible Years*, starring David Niven.

Lillie and I continued to date on and off through high school, although she broke up our exclusive relationship on a couple of occasions. I ultimately went with her to her high school prom when I was a freshman at the University of Miami. When Lillie graduated high school, she attended community college in Miami and then transferred to the University of Florida in Gainesville. After that, we fell out of touch for over three years.

Sometime during the summer of 1974, our mutual high school friend Saul Rubin asked me, "Guess who's back in town?" It was Lillie, home from college and working in the Sunny Isles section of Miami Beach at a drugstore known as Liggett's. I was now a college graduate, wore contact lenses instead of glasses, had my hair professionally cut, wore Pierre Cardin suits, and drove a new beige Pontiac Firebird with a white vinyl top. I drove over to the drugstore, and Lillie was impressed with the new Glenn.

We went out to dinner together and attended our first concert (Carole King and James Taylor at the Miami Beach Convention Center). I also got to meet her five siblings and her parents. Her mother was a professional artist, and her father was her mother's art manager. They also ran their own art gallery in Hallandale. When I met her mother, I was surprised that she spoke Spanish. Her mother had European parents who had immigrated to Cuba when they were not able to enter the United States. It was a busy household. Her parents were deeply involved in their business and making a living for everyone, and the children mostly took care of each other.

Later that summer, I arrived in Las Vegas to start working for my father at Games of Nevada, though I was unsure of what that career path would look like. "You cannot do better than working in the family business," I was often told. I was away from my home in North Miami Beach and my mother for the first protracted period in my life. On top of that, I wasn't yet sure that the life my father and mother wanted for me, as a gaming industry executive in Las Vegas, was one that I would enjoy pursuing. I also missed Lillie, and we stayed in close touch with each other. She returned to Gainesville in the fall to begin her senior year at the University of Florida, where I traveled to visit her as often as I could.

When I began working with my father at the family business, I was provided with an office and a nameplate for my desk. I had no assigned duties, no training to speak of, and no idea what I was supposed to do in return for my weekly pay-check. I was also staying at my father's house, where he lived with Zola.

Here I was, a college graduate with some skills and talents, but no outlet to apply them. My days at Games of Nevada involved reading the new *Billboard* magazine to see what the top 100 record hits were that week, counting the lines of patterns that were affixed to the four walls of my office, going to Tiffany's Cleaners in Commercial Center to deliver and pick up my father's clothes, having lunches and dinners together with my father's business friends and colleagues, and occasionally transporting guests from McCarran International Airport to their hotels. This is essentially what my job entailed for a period of three years as a full-time employee of the company.

Occasionally, my father would send me on some obscure sales or marketing mission outside Las Vegas. One time he asked me to travel to Reno to promote a new slot machine developed by the Seeburg Corporation based in Chicago. Seeburg was a jukebox company that decided to venture into the gaming industry. They developed a very attractive upright slot machine that some thought could be competitive to Bally, the majority market shareholder in the slot industry at the time. I was given a stack of one-page Seeburg slot machine brochures and directed to approach the various casinos in downtown Reno on Virginia Street.

I went door-to-door handing out the brochures to casino owners and managers. The reception was lukewarm at best until I walked into Fitzgerald's Casino and introduced the owner, Lincoln Fitzgerald, to the Seeburg company and its products. Coincidentally, and unbeknownst to me at the time, Mr. Fitzgerald was once an accountant with Seeburg and had a romantic relationship with the daughter of the original owner of the company. Allegedly, when Mr. Fitzgerald left Seeburg to relocate to Reno—along with company funds and the owner's daughter—he was targeted to be taken out. He'd survived multiple gunshot wounds and was now an older man, hunched over at the waist due to his injuries. But, knowing none of this, when Mr. Fitzgerald chased me out of his casino with a hammer in his hand, yelling at the top of his voice, I assumed that he just wasn't very impressed with the Seeburg product.

I often approached my father and asked him when I could get more involved in his business. His usual response was: "Have patience." I began questioning myself—did I see things differently than everyone else? My family members regarded me as the heir and successor to my father's business enterprise, but how could that be true if he never involved me in the business? Sure, he'd send me off on a couple of slot route collections or maybe to pass some circulars of newly developed company games to casino locations, but there was no further business involvement. I was questioning my mental health and my self-worth.

When I began to express my desire to leave Las Vegas, other family members would say, "How can you wash your hands of the family business?" Maybe they saw something that I didn't, but my father was not the type of person to delegate responsibilities to others, and I felt that I wasn't losing anything by leaving. In hindsight, I realize why my father acted the way he did during that time. While he wanted me close to him after not knowing me well during my childhood, it is likely that he didn't want me to get close to the Mob personalities involved in the gaming business during those turbulent years.

Although this wasn't a productive time in my career, I very much enjoyed the moments I spent with my father. I watched him use his inventive mind to create the next greatest gaming machines during this pre-digital era. All his games were created with physical and practical moving parts. He created such games as a dealer-assisted horse-racing machine as well as the automated Quarter Horse racing machine using a straight track and later an oval track engineered by a wonderful and charming chain-smoking engineer from Tulsa named Charlie Laughton. I watched Charlie develop the racetrack field using miniature horse figures that ran the field of the track via an underlying chain-link operating system.

My father also created an Auto Roulette game, a draw poker machine with a card-flipping device, and a simple heads or tails game with a coin that spun on a metal post that ran horizontally across the glass-enclosed playfield. He designed bingo-themed slot machines and specialty bingo air-blower games that mechanically circulated the bingo balls. The air-blower games were kind of antiquated in that the player could hear what sounded like a vacuum cleaner operating inside the electronic unit during each play. My father made a stock market–themed slot machine as well as a Social Security number slot machine (which would never be approved by regulatory authorities today due to data security issues).

His most successful invention was his Flip-It game. In this game, the player rolled coins into the game field, where they were flipped up in the air, hitting a rotating metal-blade cylinder. The coins either entered a moving field of baskets for awards or fell on a shelf with other accumulated coins, which might be pushed off to a drop location below for player winnings. At one time, he developed a low-profile slot machine with a newly styled slant that was eventually purchased by Bally and named the Bally Classic. These slot machines did not have top boxes or high back-end cabinets or displays so that security could see everyone on the casino floor. After purchasing the game and its intellectual property from my father, Bally essentially shelved the games and took them out of the industry mix of their available game models. Possibly there was a market reason for their decision to shelve the new product, but my father speculated that his design interfered with their current production and rollout plans.

He also operated a gaming route, which consisted of machines placed in many restricted gaming license locations in Las Vegas. These locations, which included Safeway supermarkets, were only approved to have fifteen or fewer gaming machines. A bank of fifteen slot machines was usually placed just beyond the checkout counter of the grocery store, and the earnings realized at these locations were steady and profitable. There was a time when the earnings dropped off significantly, although the slot machines were the same ones that we had originally placed and the level of customer traffic was the same. My father suspected that one of his route managers was stealing, but there were no security cameras overseeing collection activities in those times.

In order to investigate, my father gave each route manager a one-week paid vacation. When he saw a week where the profit margin returned to its average win, he knew who was dipping into the gaming machine collections. The individual was approached when he returned from vacation, and he subsequently left the country to avoid having criminal charges brought against him.

Every once in a while, my father was called to appear before the State of Nevada Gaming Control Board. He generally handled himself really well, with a good degree of confidence. There was one particular hearing I attended with him where he claimed he was having difficulty hearing the questions. I do believe that my father heard the questions. He probably just did not want to respond to them. My father then reached into his pocket and pulled out a set of hearing aids that he had presumably brought so he could clearly understand the questions. He picked up one of the two hearing aids and began to tweak it with his finger. It set off a loud shrill and my father just looked up at the board members and shrugged his shoulders.

Frustrated with the lack of progress, the board decided not to proceed and my father was dismissed from the hearing. In hindsight, although my father did have hearing problems, I don't recall that my father wore hearing aids.

There were two notable projects that my father engaged in with surprising results. In the early 1980s, Cadillac introduced a small version of its line of automobiles, the Cadillac Seville. To promote the car, he created a custom four-reel slot machine; if the player lined up four Cadillac Seville decals on the reels, they would win the actual car. My father worked with the local Cadillac agency, Cashman Cadillac, to supply automobiles to a casino whenever a player won. The odds of winning the primary jackpot and receiving a car were less than 1 in 15,000.

The Stardust Hotel and Casino had several carousels of these custom machines. During the first week of the slot machines being in operation, at least three Cadillac Seville automobiles were delivered to the Stardust for jackpot-winning players. I couldn't understand how three players had supposedly hit the jackpot in a week, as I assumed the math model of the game would not support such a statistical result. Years later, when I asked my father what was wrong with the games that he had manufactured, he shared with me that nothing was wrong with the games or the math model. The owners of the Stardust at the time were the same individuals depicted in the Mob-themed movie *Casino*. The bosses simply wanted to own their own Cadillac Sevilles, and that was the cost of doing business.

My father had a small workshop at 305 West Charleston in Las Vegas. It was used mostly for parts, tool and die storage, and working on occasional projects. One year, my father and his longtime friend Gabe Forman decided they wanted to replicate the manufacture of high-quality billiard balls, like the type fabricated in Belgium. Gabe and my father worked on obtaining all the powders, resins, and other ingredients necessary to create a quality set of billiard balls. After many months of working on the project, some friends were invited to witness the result. A rack of the finished billiard balls, professionally painted with stripes, numbers, and other traditional markings, was displayed on a billiard table in the shop. They looked to be of first-class quality, with a shining finish applied to each ball. Now, the finished product would be put to the test. The billiard balls were placed in a rack, a cue ball was set, and then the demonstration began. It ended just as quickly for when the cue ball hit the rack, all the billiard balls split in half. My father and Gabe had puzzled looks on their faces. The project ended then and there.

I learned of another venture that my father's friends had taken an active financial interest in. An associate of Gabe Forman and Irving Green, son of Abe Green, decided to invest in an amazing medical product developed or discovered by their business associate in Japan, whose name was Kenny. Kenny showed them a powdery substance that, when added to water and consumed, would purportedly cure most medical ailments. I don't know how far into the venture the three individuals took their business and product, but the feedback from customers was that the magic powder was not at all effective in curing their ailments.

I assume that my father was approached by Kenny to make an investment in the venture, but my father was suspicious about the validity of the product. He obtained a sample and requested a research lab at the University of Nevada, Las Vegas, to analyze its composition. The research lab's report stated that the powder was entirely composed of dirt. The venture ended, and Kenny was henceforth called the Sandman.

I was traveling to Florida often to visit with Lillie, and by Christmas 1975, I had asked her if she would consider spending her winter break with me in Las Vegas. She agreed, and our family friend Rick Schwartz made his townhouse available for us to stay in together. Lillie and I had a wonderful time in Las Vegas, which also included a trip to Los Angeles to stay at the Beverly Hilton, dine at Dan Tana's in Beverly Hills next door to the famous Troubadour nightclub, and travel up the coast to visit the Dutch-themed town of Solvang. For someone who had grown up in Florida and not been to the West Coast before, it was quite an experience for her to take in the desert landscape in Nevada and the changing scenery while driving over mountain passes on our way to Southern California.

Upon returning to Las Vegas just before New Year's Eve, Lillie asked if we could see a show to celebrate the New Year. Getting a show reservation on short notice in Las Vegas on New Year's Eve was not an easy task, but my father made it happen. He called his dear friend Mannie Halbert, who owned the Raleigh Hotel in the Catskill Mountains of New York. Mannie called his brother-in-law, who was a very well-known booking agent in the entertainment industry. By New Year's Eve, Lillie and I had reservations to see the comedian Totie Fields, who was appearing in the Congo Room at the Sahara Hotel. And this wasn't just any reservation, it was for a two-seated cocktail table stage right.

Lillie returned to the University of Florida to complete her senior year after our Las Vegas holiday. I traveled to visit her during the spring semester of 1975, and we drove to Cedar Key to spend a weekend together. The drive from Gainesville to Cedar Key was about one hour. While driving there, I was feeling anxious about asking her a question. We arrived at Cedar Key and took a walk along the beachfront. When I felt the right moment, I turned to Lillie.

"Would you go steady with me?" I asked, meaning would she date me exclusively.

She hesitated for about five seconds and then responded with a grin, "Would you instead marry me?"

To say that I was stunned was an understatement. My

heart began to race. "Yes!" I immediately answered. I was so happy—my feelings expanded beyond any words I could use to express them.

While I figured this was better than just going steady, I also realized that my career had not truly developed to where I felt financially secure enough to get married. I called my father later that day and told him about Lillie's proposal (which I had already accepted), hoping for his approval. My father wanted to see me happy, but he also wanted me to stay in Las Vegas, so he simply said, "Glenn, I am fine with you getting married to Lillie. Just don't have children right away."

I later procured an engagement ring for Lillie. After some deliberation together, Lillie agreed to move to Las Vegas and live with me following her college graduation. We ended up moving to and then away from Las Vegas three times over a two-year period. We first lived together in Las Vegas from our engagement in September 1975 until June 1976, when we moved back to Florida and were married at Temple Israel in downtown Miami.

We spent our honeymoon on the East Coast, road-tripping from South Florida up to New England. On our way, we stopped in Hurleyville, where I introduced Lillie to some of the members of my father's family. We also visited the family bakery. We then traveled to Boston, visiting several historical colonial sites, and ultimately made our way up the Maine coast as far north as Bar Harbor. We enjoyed sampling the delicious lobster and seafood of the area while becoming enamored of the quaint coastal towns of Kennebunkport and Ogunquit. When we finally returned to South Florida, it was time for us to consider how to begin charting our lives and future together.

Following our wedding and honeymoon, my father asked me if I would try to work in the business with him a second time. I still wasn't sure that was what I wanted, but I did need a job. We decided to try living in Las Vegas again, now as a married couple, to see if the situation would change. Lillie and I drove our two fully packed cars across the country from Miami to Las Vegas, keeping in touch with each other via our citizens band (CB) radios. This was a time many years before cell phones, but it was fun making the journey together and calling out to each other by radio using our CB handles: White Bird (for me, named after my white Pontiac Firebird) and Dandelion (which was a favorite flower of Lillie's).

The cross-country drive was always enjoyable, the scenery spectacular. However, once we crossed over Hoover Dam and entered Nevada, a heavy feeling of despair set in. I sensed that our return to Las Vegas would be a repeat of the last time I lived there—just another failed attempt to work in the family business. It was wonderful having Lillie with me this time, though; she gave me strength to see things through and do the best that we could for each other.

As I feared, this attempt was a repeat of the first. We lived in an apartment complex on Valley View Boulevard near the intersection of West Sahara Avenue. Lillie spent her time working as a volunteer with the local suicide hotline after having been a caseworker at Nevada State Welfare in nearby Henderson during our previous attempt to stay rooted in Las Vegas. When our apartment lease was up, we decided to return to Miami even though I was still on the company payroll. Nothing had changed in my career path with my father. I was so frustrated and could not understand why I was being asked to work in the family business and gain a better understanding of how it operated but was given no real role or duties.

When we returned to Miami, we lived with my mother and her husband, Kap, for a few months while trying to find some viable career path forward for both of us. After I was unsuccessful in finding meaningful employment in South Florida, my father made one more attempt and asked me to try working with him a third time. While Lillie and I were hesitant, we again made the cross-country trip to Las Vegas—this time checking into a motel rather than signing an apartment lease. We ate breakfasts of cold cereal in our room using cooking pots instead of dishes, and we had only a couple of spoons and forks to work with.

My mother always supported my father's efforts to lure me back to Las Vegas because she assumed it provided me with a financially sound future. Lillie was on my side and could not understand why my father would not give me an opportunity to learn the business and participate in it in any meaningful way. One day during this last attempt, Lillie approached my father and, plainly frustrated, asked, "Why don't you give Glenn a chance?"

While I am sure that financial security was important to Lillie, as it would be to any newly married spouse, I believe she saw my dismay and distress. I simply did not see a future for myself in the family business, and I was beginning to have significant self-esteem issues. I ultimately decided that I could not play this game anymore and had to find some independent career path to pursue for my own mental health, the health of my new marriage, the security of my future family, and the direction of my life. We left Las Vegas and returned to Florida just three weeks later.

CHAPTER 9

Five Years of Law School

Lillie and I returned to my home in North Miami Beach by the spring of 1977 with the realization that we both needed to seek new career paths. Living and working in Nevada with my father was a nonstarter, three times, and as frustrating as those experiences were, they brought clarity to my need to move forward in my life outside the family business.

I began a job search in Miami and quickly found that my bachelor of arts degree in political science was of little use in seeking a new career. One successful interview offered me a position selling ads in *The Yellow Pages*—a physical business directory prevalent in pretech times. The base salary would be $7,500 per year. The interviewer asked if I knew what "software" was, and I honestly didn't. I knew what "silverware" was, but that was as close an understanding as I had of software in the mid-1970s.

After a few weeks of living in my childhood home, Lillie pressed upon me that it was time for us to get our own apartment. We signed a lease for a one-bedroom in a complex called

Buttonwood, which was on Kendall Drive in South Miami. We began to furnish the apartment, and just three weeks into the lease, I received a call from my father. He said he had heard about a new law school opening in Southern California, and it was accepting applications for late admission. When my father asked if I would be interested, I said yes and shared the conversation with Lillie. I guess my father finally realized that I would not be making another attempt at working in the family business in Las Vegas, and I appreciated his continuing support.

Somehow, we were able to break our apartment lease and just lose our security deposit. Before long, I traveled to Los Angeles and began looking for an apartment in the San Fernando Valley, where the law school was. Claudia met me in Los Angeles and found an apartment complex that looked good to me: Oakwood Garden Apartments on Sherman Way in Van Nuys. I told Lillie about it, and she then flew across the country to move into our new apartment in California.

I vividly recall Lillie's expression upon seeing the actual apartment in person.

"You can't be serious!" she said, chuckling in disbelief.

The apartment was on a main street with the noise of the city, the sirens of the fire engines, and plenty of soot to sweep off the living room's outdoor patio every day. The oven in the small kitchen *might* have held a frozen preprepared dinner. This became home for us for the next few months.

I was quickly accepted into the Valley University School of Law, and I began my studies in North Hollywood on the corner of Riverside and Lankershim. It was a start-up that had rented facilities and contracted with a bookmobile that would drive by once a week to provide textbooks. The law school was not approved by the American Bar Association, but we were told it would be reviewed for accreditation the following year.

I enjoyed my studies, and Lillie kept busy with her new girlfriend Sara Goldberg, experiencing the sights and sounds of Los Angeles. Sara's husband, Steve, was a friend of mine at the law school, and like us, they had moved to Los Angeles from the East Coast in search of a new start.

After a few months, we found out that the law school was not moving toward accreditation as they had previously represented to us. The school was running out of operating funds and ultimately closed by the end of the year. Steve and I demanded to know what their intention was for those of us who had moved across the country to attend a law school whose accreditation status had been misrepresented. They responded through their attorney by issuing certified letters to me and Steve, threatening us with legal action for defamation of character against the dean if we did not cease and desist. Not wanting to get involved in litigation, I just had to accept the fact that Lillie and I needed to reconsider what to do and where to go next.

I applied for admission to two fully accredited law schools in San Diego and Sacramento, while Lillie applied to graduate schools in the same cities with hopes of pursuing a master's degree in social work. I was fortunate to be invited to an admission interview at the University of the Pacific, McGeorge School of Law, in Sacramento. McGeorge was a prominent law school and fully approved by the American Bar Association (ABA). This meant that upon graduating and obtaining my juris doctor degree, I could sit for any state bar examination in the United States. Although I did not fully apply myself in my undergraduate studies, my grades for the first year of law school in North Hollywood provided a basis for more serious consideration by the McGeorge School of Law.

Lillie and I flew to Sacramento and found a very beautiful city lined with bike paths and surrounded by nature—very different from where we had lived before. I went to the law school for my interview appointment with Associate Dean Ryan.

"Here's the thing, Glenn," he said. "The law school would

like to consider your admission for the part-time evening division with classes beginning in a month." I thought about a part-time law school program. The credits I earned in my year in North Hollywood would not transfer because they were from a non-ABA law school. Four more years of law school just seemed like an eternity to commit to in order to obtain my law degree.

"Is there any chance you'll reconsider and allow me to attend the full-time day program at McGeorge?"

He stared at me with a very straight and firm expression on his face and uttered these memorable words: "We would rather see you as a graduate than a casualty."

My only option was to accept admittance for the part-time evening program at McGeorge.

Law school was not easy, and McGeorge was known to have a high attrition rate among incoming students. But I was committed. Lillie and I found a beautiful apartment in an expansive garden-like complex in Sacramento called Woodside. We moved up from Los Angeles, and I began classes at McGeorge in June 1978. At the same time, Lillie was accepted to California State University in Sacramento, also known as Sac State, to work toward a two-year master's degree in social work. My father made this all financially possible for us, and I am eternally grateful to him for his understanding and support. It was now up to me to learn how to study and invest serious time and hours toward my coursework, and to ultimately succeed in earning my juris doctor degree.

I felt I could not afford to fail as I had nothing to fall back on. I studied many hours while also working, at different times, as a legislative assistant at the California State Legislature, a law clerk for the presiding judge of the Sacramento Superior Court, and a supervised law student assisting claimants in a Small Claims Advisory Clinic at the county courthouse. Once

Lillie graduated, she began working at the Alta California Regional Center.

We had less free time to travel and visit family due to our intense study and job requirements, but we did stay in touch with family, my father in particular. One day, he called and asked if we wanted to get away for a long weekend in Los Angeles because he would like to meet us there. We told him we would meet him on his arrival at the Los Angeles International Airport. While my father financially supported us to a significant degree during our schooling, we didn't want him to have to assume other unnecessary expenses. We thought we would surprise him by driving down from Sacramento and picking him up at the airport.

Lillie and I awaited his arrival outside the terminal. When he emerged, he was shocked we had driven our car some seven hours to pick him up. He had reserved a Rolls-Royce limo to take us on a spoiling experience at L'Ermitage, a high-end boutique hotel in Beverly Hills. Lillie quickly walked away from our old Chevy Monte Carlo and got into the Rolls-Royce to travel to the hotel with my father, while I followed in the Chevy. He always made every effort for us.

We all stayed at L'Ermitage for a long weekend. The rooms were exquisite in design and presentation, with finishing touches of an in-room fireplace and a basketful of expensive perfume samples. My father handed me some cash and suggested I walk nearby to Robertson's department store to purchase appropriate evening clothing for Lillie. We had dinner in Beverly Hills with my father's friends from the Catskills, Mannie and Nettie Halbert, owners of the Raleigh Hotel. Some celebrities were also dining, and there was mutual recognition between Mannie and Nettie and a couple of the Jewish entertainers who had begun their careers at Catskills hotels. That relaxing, high-class weekend was a vacation we treasured during a time in life when we weren't getting many breaks.

Following the completion of my third year of evening classes at McGeorge, it seemed I might actually graduate and become an attorney in the next year. A law student at McGeorge would never know for sure. The students were tacitly influenced by the school to be highly competitive with each other. The implied statement was: "Look to the left of you, and look to the right of you. At the end of this school year, one of you won't be here." Many students did not achieve the grades necessary to continue in their legal education, and only the cream of the crop survived to eventually take the bar exam.

The law school experience always had me on edge as I didn't know what tomorrow would bring or how I would overcome academic challenges. But with the third year of law school education behind me, Lillie and I began to relax, and we decided to spend the $5,000 we had in savings on something worthwhile. We talked about buying our own furniture instead of renting it and considered other domestic ideas. We decided instead to go on an amazing trip together. Lillie went to River City Travel in Sacramento to inquire about foreign travel. Our travel agent informed her of a group trip being organized to visit the People's Republic of China. We decided to explore a new world that was foreign to most Americans who were born after the Chinese Revolution of 1949.

We drove to San Francisco, parked our car in a long-term lot, and boarded a Boeing 747 aircraft that had "CAAC" on its body. The initials stood for the Civil Aviation Administration of China. We embarked on an amazing journey with twenty-five other Americans traveling under a group visa. We were some of the younger passengers on the trip, which also included senior citizens, doctors, and actors who were traveling to China to film a movie. We met actress June Lockhart as well as the CBS 60 *Minutes* investigative reporter Mike Wallace.

It was a unique opportunity to experience China post-revolution when its doors were slightly opening again to foreigners. Many men were still wearing the old Mao military jackets and revolutionary hats with the red star during our visit. We toured Beijing, Nanjing, Suzhou, Hangzhou, and Shanghai and visited schools and tea farms, saw pandas in the Beijing Zoo, traveled down the Yangtze River, ate yellow seedless watermelon, and walked on the Great Wall of China. After close to three weeks of exploring in China, it was time to head back home to California and resume our schooling and work in Sacramento.

CHAPTER 10

An Invitation from the White House

One of the highlights of my law school career was having the opportunity to intern as a legislative assistant for the majority floor leader of the California State Assembly, Assemblyman Mike Roos of Los Angeles. This was an intern opportunity through the McGeorge clinical program for attending law students. By working in a clinical school program, I was rewarded with semester credits upon completion of the internship rather than receiving compensation from the state. I worked at the California State Capitol for over a year assisting Assemblyman Roos and his staff as he sponsored and supported various assembly bills to address the issue of crime in the community. I recall a favorite political statement used during those years in the California legislature that "we must examine the root causes of crime." It sounded good politically, but society is still trying to address the abhorrent level of crime in American society today.

I met various state-elected officials at the start of their political careers who later became members of Congress and the United States Senate. Willie Brown was the Speaker of the California Assembly and later became mayor of San Francisco for many years. Maxine Waters was also a member of the State Assembly, and she is now a prominent member of Congress. I very much enjoyed my time interning in the California legislature, and the experience piqued my interest in the legislative process and public office.

Assemblyman Roos wanted to express his personal gratitude to me for the work that I accomplished with his staff during my tenure in his office, so one day we met in his legislative office in Sacramento.

"Glenn, do you have any plans or career interests now that you are graduating law school?" he asked.

"I have always wanted to pursue a career in government service in Washington, DC," I said.

"I have a good friend and colleague who is a cabinet secretary in the White House," he said. "Would you mind if I made an inquiry for you?"

"Absolutely! And thank you!" I replied.

Within a couple of weeks, I received a copy of a letter that the assemblyman had sent to Craig Fuller, the cabinet secretary to Vice President George H. W. Bush during the Reagan presidency. The letter expressed my interest in serving in a career position in federal service. Shortly thereafter, I received a letter from Secretary Fuller inviting me to the West Wing of the White House, along with follow-up meetings and interviews.

With much excitement and anticipation, I traveled to Washington, DC, and checked into the Hotel Washington, just a few blocks from the president's home. The next morning, I received a call from the White House instructing me when and where to enter the premises for my meeting. It was a breezy day, and the American flag flew prominently above the iconic building as I walked up to the northwest gate. I approached security, provided my identification, and was issued a pass to enter the White House. I walked toward the double doors of the West Wing in disbelief. A US Marine in full uniform opened the door for me with white-gloved hands. I was led inside to the waiting area, given a glass of Coke at my request, and then ushered into Secretary Fuller's office. It was a cordial meeting, and I expressed my appreciation to him for meeting with me.

After about twenty minutes, I was escorted to the Office of Presidential Personnel in the adjoining Eisenhower Executive Office Building for a personal interview. This office is responsible for vetting new political appointees. They asked me questions about my career path and desires and my educational background. One question of note was whom did I support in the last presidential election. I responded: "The president, of course." The current president was Ronald Reagan. I had actually supported and voted for the prior sitting president, Jimmy Carter, but that seemed like the wrong answer. When the interview concluded, I was told that I should expect to hear from their office and that they would maintain contact with me. I left the White House grounds and returned to my hotel room, the exciting events of the day in my mind on repeat. The next morning, I flew back home to Sacramento.

My father was able to arrange for and provide the White House with a support letter for my consideration penned by Nevada's governor Paul Laxalt. Governor Laxalt and President Reagan were very close friends and political allies. In his letter, Governor Laxalt stated that although I attended law school for eleven months of each calendar year and was unable to be actively involved in the Reagan for President campaign, he verified that I was a full supporter of President Reagan.

Of course, I had been a lifelong Democrat and did not

support President Reagan or the Republican ticket. I guess the governor assumed I had supported President Reagan as my father was continuing to financially contribute to both sides of the aisle while also pulling his own strings of influence. As my father would often say: "Don't waste your silver bullet." Well, he used one for me in this instance. I continued to hear from the Office of Presidential Personnel for the next few months while I awaited some hopeful news about my desire to enter federal service in Washington, DC.

Above: My grandparents Louis and Ethel Pesekow with one of their children in the mid-1930s, when they founded Pesekow's Bungalow Colony in Loch Sheldrake, New York.
Left: My parents, Michael "Mickey" Wichinsky and Ann (Pesekow) Wichinsky, at Pesekow's Bungalow Colony in 1949.

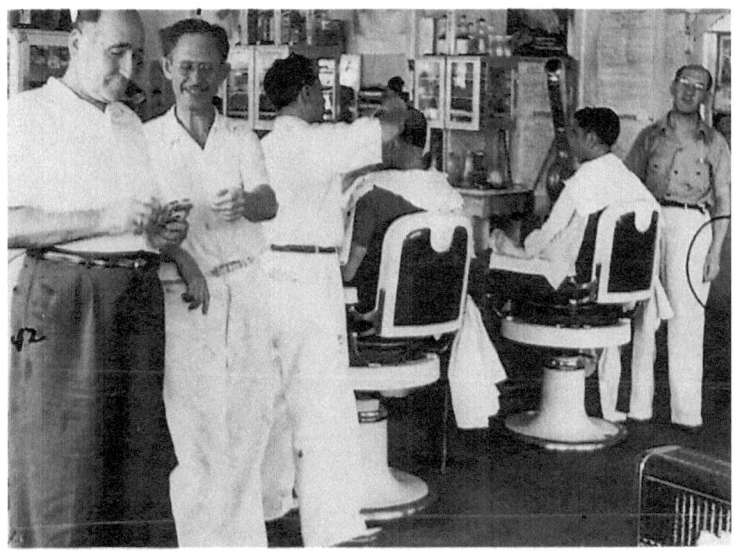

Second from the left: My grandfather Louis Pesekow, barber, Loch Sheldrake, New York, mid- to late 1940s.

My grandparents Ethel and Louis Pesekow, at right, at Pesekow's Bungalow Colony in the late 1950s or early 1960s.

My uncle Nate Wichinsky (second from left) with friends, after enlisting for military service in WWII. (Note the framed picture of Douglas MacArthur on the wall behind them.)

My uncle Louis "Lebel" Wichinsky, inventor of the first patented bagel machine, which could produce six hundred bagels an hour, in Hurleyville, New York.

Above: Me in front of Wichinsky's Bake Shop in Hurleyville, New York, at a young age. Left: My parents at their wedding reception in 1945 with "Grandpa Jake," my grandfather Jacob Wichinsky.

*Above: My parents in New York, around 1950. Below: My dad and David ("Gabe")
Forman on Miami Beach in the early 1960s.*

Me with my dad at my bar mitzvah reception at the Raleigh Hotel in South Fallsburg, New York, summer 1966.

The famous Sands Hotel in Las Vegas.

The "Rat Pack" in front of the Sands Hotel sign on the Las Vegas Strip.

Above: Abe Green with one of his Runyon Sales distributors in New Jersey. I was told the gentleman on the right was later terminated. Below: Victor Tsao with my dad and my cousin Steve Kaufman at Games of Nevada, 1972.

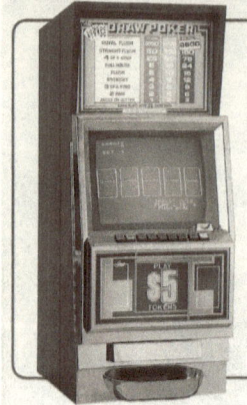

JUMBO VIDEO POKER
(GVP-10)

GAMES OF NEVADA'S Jumbo Video Poker offers all the features of the GVP7A and more.

The extra large capacity hopper minimizes hand pays. Progressive system optional. All denominations, including special gaming tokens $5 and $25.

Dimensions: Height: 50" — Width: 21¼" — Depth: 24"

CASINO ROYAL DRAW POKER
(GCR)

GAMES OF NEVADA'S Casino Royal features the added realism of real cards being shuffled. You still have the video poker speed but without monitor glare and eye fatigue.

This game features modular stepper motors for reliability and ease of service, and a 7" non-glare CRT to monitor all bets and payouts. Credit feature, last-two-game recall, complete accountability are standard. All denominations.

We feature all standard pay schedules including "10's or Better." Progressive system optional.

Dimensions: Height: 33½" — Width: 17¼" — Depth: 24"

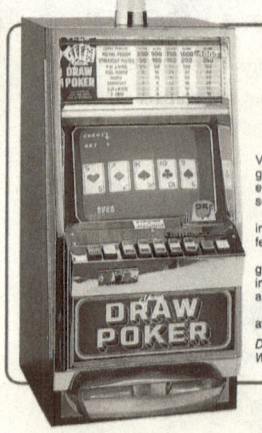

VIDEO DRAW POKER
(GVP7A)

GAMES OF NEVADA'S Video Draw Poker (7A) offers greater player appeal through enhanced graphics and screen resolution.

All standard pay schedules including "10's or Better" are featured.

Credit feature, last-two-game recall, customized playing cards, and complete accountability are standard. Progressive systems available. All denominations.

Dimensions: Height: 33½" — Width: 17¼" — Depth: 24"

Three models of video poker games developed and manufactured by my father's company, Games of Nevada. Games of Nevada was an independent and licensed manufacturer, distributor, and operator of electronic gaming machines. The company was founded by my father in the early 1970s, in Las Vegas, Nevada.

FAST ACTION MINI KENO

GAMES OF NEVADA'S Mini Keno is a totally new, innovative and simplified approach to Keno.

The play and appearance of this fast action game is so close to Keno that it will gain immediate recognition and acceptance by the Keno playing customer, and is attractive enough to create new Mini Keno players, especially with a $12,000 top prize (quarter machine).

This game features a wide variety of payout schedules including 8 spot 8, 9 spot 9, and 10 spot 10 progressive jackpots.

The artwork and animation speak for themselves. Credit, last-two-game recall, and complete accountability are standard.

Denominations: 5¢ and 25¢.

Dimensions: Height: 33½" — Width: 17¼" — Depth: 24"

DOUBLE SCREEN KENO
(GVK-2)

GAMES OF NEVADA now offers this sleek, two-screen Keno machine with comfort touch panel, enhanced graphics and screen resolution.

Machine mounts conveniently on 24" wide stand, saving casino floor space.

Our Double Screen Keno features a wide array of payout schedules including 8 spot 8, 9 spot 9, and 10 spot 10 progressive jackpots.

Credit feature, last-two-game recall is optional. Denominations: 5¢ and 25¢.

Dimensions: Height: 48" — Width: 17¼" — Depth: 22½"

Two models of electronic keno machines developed and manufactured by Games of Nevada.

Two bright and shiny faces beam out at visitors to the recent International Gaming Business Exposition. The one on the right belongs to Michael "Mickey" Wichinsky, president of Games of Nevada. The face on the left is one of the better ideas out of Mickey's company, a slot machine with card faces that actually flip during the cycling, much as the old card-flips of the late 1800s. This updated, old-favorite format got a lot of attention at the show because of its unique operation.

My dad exhibiting one of his gaming machines at an international gaming exposition in London in 1986.

A rare photo of my parents together, at a family event in Las Vegas, 1997.

CHAPTER 11

Is There Life After Law School?

Law school studies were very intense, and the professors and school administration would never suggest that you might one day successfully complete your studies and become an attorney. In fact, the student bookstore sold bumper stickers that asked: "Is There Life After Law School?"

I put everything into my studies, taking notes to summarize all my readings and preparing for each class so I could recite the Issue, Rule, Analysis, and Conclusion (IRAC) for each assigned case. I also strategized that if I signed up for the maximum number of pass/fail courses, which did not assign a grade, I had a much better chance of finishing my law school studies with a passing grade point average.

Ultimately, in May 1982, I successfully completed my studies at the University of the Pacific McGeorge School of Law in Sacramento and was conferred my juris doctor degree in the top 20 percent of my class. It was a long five-year academic journey, but I finally attained an advanced degree I could now put to constructive use.

Six months later, Lillie and I had another wonderful benchmark in our lives with the birth of our daughter, Laura. Laura was born in American River Hospital in Sacramento through natural childbirth, and I cut the umbilical cord. There were no formalities, no medications or spinal blocks involved, and the song "Southern Cross" sung by Crosby, Stills & Nash was playing when Laura came into this world and our family. She gave us happiness from day one and brought a greater closeness to our marriage.

It was our intention to move back to Florida after I completed law school, so I had spent the summer studying for the Florida Bar examination. While Lillie and I liked California and would have considered staying there, the California Bar examination had a pass rate of 33 percent, and I didn't want to fail my first try at becoming a licensed attorney. I was successful in my first attempt to receive my Florida Bar attorney license and was now officially an attorney, but my first real job was as a stay-at-home dad while Lillie went back to work. I spent my time with Laura reading books, playing with toys, and watching many episodes of *Sesame Street*. Laura was a big fan of Big Bird and the other characters.

During this time, I sent out résumés seeking my first law position, but things only happen in their own time. I also continued to receive calls from the Office of Presidential Personnel to check on my status and availability during late fall and early winter. However, on one status call, I was asked what I was engaged in during the workday. I stated I was at home taking care of our newborn while my wife was at work. Well, I guess such honesty about being a stay-at-home dad was not politically correct in the early 1980s. I never heard from the White House again.

Despite that disappointment, I was still interested in

government service. But I needed a job and began applying earnestly for law firm positions as a law clerk or as an incoming associate. One day, I saw a listing on the law school job board on campus for a career in federal government service with the Central Intelligence Agency (CIA). I assumed the agency was seeking attorney recruits to support the legal needs of the CIA. I applied for a position and some weeks later was invited to be interviewed by the agency.

I drove to the San Francisco Federal Building downtown. On the thirteenth floor, I buzzed the designated room and was let in. The first thing I saw was a bald eagle fixture prominently displayed above the second doorframe with the official markings of the CIA.

I soon learned that the position I thought I was applying for was very different from what the agency had in mind for me. The agent thanked me for my interest in joining the CIA.

"We are interested in your candidacy with the CIA as a member of our covert division," said the agent. He knew that I had recently visited the People's Republic of China, so he asked if I was proficient in Mandarin; I told him I was not.

"Do you have conversational Spanish?" he asked.

"I did study Spanish from grade school through college, but I haven't spoken Spanish much in the past few years. I am sure I could improve it," I replied.

The agent continued. "Based upon your knowledge and prior language skills in Spanish, we would like you to consider joining our agency to be trained for covert activities in Nicaragua. You will not use your law degree in this position, and you will need to behave more like a used car salesman in your daily assignments. We will settle you in Nicaragua, and you'll be paid a starting salary of $21,500 with benefits."

I realized this offer was even less than I would have earned if I had become a meteorologist, which was originally my chosen career path. I asked about security and risks to my life in such a position, but was told these issues hardly ever occur. We closed the meeting with his suggestion that I sit for some psychological testing for the position.

I drove back to Sacramento, shared the experience with Lillie, and the next day sent a one-line letter to the agent stating that I was not interested in pursuing the offered position with the CIA. I was seeking a stable job and career with a decent income, not one that would entail me risking my life. I decided that perhaps it was best to focus on career opportunities outside government service.

CHAPTER 12

Investing in the Nevada Gaming Industry

I soon discovered that my days of limited involvement with the family business were not over.

In 1979, my father asked my sister and me to apply for Nevada gaming licenses in order to become shareholders in Westronics, a closely held corporation in Nevada. My father and other associates were the shareholders in this company, but some of the shareholders who were former Bally officials were leaving and selling their shares back to the company. My father made these shares available to my sister and me.

My father retained the legal services of Robert Faiss to represent Claudia and me in the regulatory process. Bob was an upstanding gaming attorney and highly praised for his talents, ethics, and proven abilities. He was also one of the kindest individuals I have ever known.

Bob began the licensing process by reviewing our personal and financial histories, the primary basis of a gaming regulatory licensing investigation. It is pretty much an open-book disclosure where you provide as much information as possible, so long as it is remotely relevant to the question posed.

One question on the application asked whether the applicant had ever been questioned by a federal, state, or local law enforcement agency. Bob knew me very well and considered my background and character to be spotless. As he proceeded to answer no to the question of my ever being questioned by a law enforcement agency, I interrupted and told him that I had once been questioned. He looked surprised and asked me to tell him more.

When I was in my early teens, I had a hobby known as shortwave listening. During this time before the computer and technology age of today, listening to the radio gave me the opportunity to hear foreign radio stations from around the world and learn more about their countries. Today, of course, we all easily connect to radio, television, cable, and other broadcast channels over the internet.

As part of this hobby, I wrote letters to radio stations, telling them of the program content, date, and time that I listened in, along with information about how weak or strong their transmission signal was at my location. In return, the radio station would confirm the information provided and then send a verification card, known as a QSL card, which would certify that I heard their radio broadcast on the date and time indicated. I displayed these verification cards, which featured a picture of the country or city where the broadcast originated from, on a bulletin board on my bedroom wall.

On one late evening, I received and listened to a radio broadcast originating from Radio Beijing in China. After listening for a while to their English-based broadcast, I thought it would be a great addition to my collection of QSL verification cards. It should be noted that, at this time, the United States and the People's Republic of China had no formal diplomatic relations with each other and there was a near-total lack of interaction between the countries. I prepared my information and mailed my request for a QSL card to Beijing.

A few weeks later, I received a QSL card from Radio Beijing confirming that I had received their broadcast. It was a colorful card with a depiction of their leader, Mao Zedong, and the Red Guards who had taken power over Mainland China and installed Communist rule over the country following World War II. But that wasn't the end of it. I soon received an English-language copy of the Little Red Book, which contained the ideology and teachings of Mao Zedong, a lapel pin with his depiction on it, and magazines about the Communist vision for living life in China as a true revolutionary. Depictions of Red Guard soldiers shooting their rifles had the bullets hitting their intended target, the president of the United States. My mother became concerned as I kept receiving more and more Communist propaganda in the mail. By this time, my mail was being opened, inspected, and then sealed before each delivery by the US Postal Service.

My mother said to me at the time that this didn't look good. Being in this precarious position in the eyes of the government could affect my life and future. So, one morning, she made an appointment for us to travel to the Miami field office of the Federal Bureau of Investigation (FBI) with all these unsolicited materials and speak with an agent. I explained to the agent what had occurred, that I had only requested the QSL card from Radio Beijing and that I wanted it noted I was not some type of Communist subversive that the government should have to keep on their watch list. An official FBI file was voluntarily opened.

At my gaming license interview, Bob Faiss said it was very unlikely this would come up in a gaming license hearing, but having said so, he would footnote the application and disclose the information along with an asterisk. A few months later, when the licensing background investigation was completed and a recommendation was made to the regulators, the first of two hearings was held on the intended Westronics equity transfer to Claudia and me.

During the first hearing before the State of Nevada Gaming Control Board, the chairman of the board, Roger Trounday, stated how impressed he was that I had conducted a research study in college regarding legalized gaming as my senior thesis in the Political Science department at the University of Miami, and also that the study had been published. It felt good to receive this positive recognition, and the three-person board all voted in favor of my licensure.

One week after the first hearing, I was required to appear before the Nevada Gaming Commission, which would then rule upon the recommendation of the Gaming Control Board. The chairman of the Nevada Gaming Commission, Harry Reid, was an emerging figure in politics. He went on to become a United States senator for Nevada and majority floor leader. Since Chairman Trounday was so kind and supportive of me in the first hearing, I was hoping for a similar reception from the Gaming Commission.

I was called to the podium and joined by my attorney, Bob Faiss. This hearing was also being broadcast on statewide television. I was then sworn in before providing testimony. Chairman Reid opened with a memorable question to me: "Mr. Wichinsky, is it true that when you were fourteen years old, you received Communist propaganda in the mail from Red China?" Bob Faiss and I were equally shocked and amazed by this opening question. I was shaking in place before the podium and was only able to utter the response: "Yes, sir, yes, sir."

My sister joked with me about my response in a playful way for many years. It was apparent that Chairman Reid wanted to make a spectacle about my honest disclosure and get a rise from the audience at my expense. Most importantly, however, the commission accepted the recommendation of the Gaming Control Board and approved our licensing applications. From that day forward, though, I haven't been a big fan of Harry Reid, and now that the airport in Las Vegas has been renamed in his memory, I just call it the Las Vegas airport.

Around this time, my father approached me with a business opportunity. A gaming route company known as Alstate Coin was selling off its route assets and seeking licensed buyers. One of the locations was a brand-name motel in Las Vegas where Alstate had been operating fifty gaming machines in the lobby. Since I was licensed, it would not be a difficult exercise to apply for another nonrestricted gaming license, which would consist of a regulatory update on my personal history, personal financial disclosures, and a review of the gaming business opportunity that I would be seeking licensure for. I had no problem being granted a second nonrestricted gaming license, which would be the second of over eight gaming licenses I would receive during my career in Nevada.

The business asset acquisition required the payment of $50,000 to Alstate Coin for their contractual position with the property owner. My father loaned me the funds to close on the transaction, and in 1982, I became a general partner of a small casino operation in Las Vegas. The contractual basis with the property owner was a simple one. They would provide the seven hundred square feet of lobby and bar space, and I would provide the gaming equipment. Our expenses related to marketing, general business administration, and payroll for three or four people who exchanged dollar bills into coins for playing the gaming devices. In later years, the gaming industry would introduce ticket-in ticket-out technology (known as TITO), which replaced coin entry and provided players with redeemable bar-coded tickets, allowing a player to play one or more gaming devices in a casino location.

The investment was a successful one, and I was able to repay my father's loan in less than six months. The casino partnership began targeting their marketing to the residents who lived within a short distance of the motel with promotions for gaming and inexpensive meals. By doing so, we were able to keep a steady stream of business coming into the location during the weekdays, which was supplemented by weekend tourists driving in from Los Angeles. The partnership continued for twenty years.

CHAPTER 13

Joining My First
Law Firm

While the business transaction had closed and my gaming license was now in place, I still pursued my legal career. There is always risk in an investment with no guarantee of continuing income or success. Lillie and I were still living in Sacramento but were open-minded to career opportunities elsewhere, should they arise.

I had to physically print out cover letters and résumés to send to prospective employers by regular mail, which made applying for jobs a tedious process, often with very long response times. I decided to stop by my law school and again view the job opportunities posted at the career placement office. A Nevada law firm was seeking an associate to engage in the field of communications law and to work in their offices in Las Vegas. The first part of the description was interesting to me, but the Las Vegas relocation was already causing some uneasiness in my stomach. I applied anyway just to see where it could lead.

A couple of weeks after applying for the position, I received a call inviting me to interview at the law firm of Rogers, Monsey, Woodbury, Phillips, Perry and Berggreen. The firm was large by Nevada standards at the time, with twenty-five partners and associates. The interview went well, and I was offered an opportunity to begin my legal career with the firm.

I had mixed feelings about returning to Las Vegas, but Lillie was encouraging. She flew ahead with Laura to a rental home that we had secured on the east side of town. I drove from Sacramento to Las Vegas with some of our belongings and our cat, Sammy. Along the way, I checked into a motel in Bakersfield, California, and called Lillie.

"I should be in Las Vegas sometime tomorrow," I told her, "but I have this gut feeling it isn't going to be a good move for us. I think it's going to be a big mistake." Just saying this brought tears to my eyes. I'd had too many life chapters in Las Vegas with disappointing outcomes, and I couldn't imagine another one.

We talked it through some more on the phone, and Lillie said, "Let's give it another try together and see how it works out."

After the call, I tried to convince myself that this was the right choice; it offered a steady income and would launch a legal career that I had worked so hard to attain. With Lillie's encouragement, I continued the journey the next morning.

Having passed the Nevada Bar exam on the first try, I began working for the law firm in 1983. I was provided with a large and finely furnished office and introduced to the staff. The senior partner, Jim Rogers, was also the owner of Valley Broadcasting Company, which owned and operated the NBC-TV affiliate station channel 3 in Las Vegas. I was looking

forward to working with him and the TV station on communications law matters.

On my second day, I was handed my first batch of files.
They all consisted of personal injury cases—this wasn't what
I had signed up for. I asked what had happened to the communications law issues I was told I would be handling. I was
informed that a current associate of the firm favored by the
senior partner would be handling those matters. I felt the job
opportunity had been clearly misrepresented to me, and I was
not happy, to say the least. I would never have chosen to relocate my family to Las Vegas to pursue a career path in personal
injury law. While I stayed with the firm for about a year, it just
wasn't a good fit and Lillie was not happy living in Las Vegas
again. We began considering a return to Sacramento or possibly moving back to our home state of Florida.

My father didn't want me to go back to the East Coast, so
he suggested we consider Reno. He had a Reno office for Games
of Nevada operated by my cousin, Steve Kaufman, and said he
could also refer me to many business clients to assist me in
developing a viable legal practice there. Since I was already a
licensed attorney in Nevada, we decided to make the attempt.

I traveled to Reno and stayed with my cousin Steve and
his wife, Sheila, while I engaged a Realtor. The Realtor found
a beautiful new home that had been built just nine months
before with only one prior owner. It was simply an amazing
house in southwest Reno on a bluff overlooking the valley. It
was Tudor-style in the front and had a ranch home patio design in the back. There were no other adjoining homes in this
new development, and it was situated on undeveloped land. I
asked Lillie to meet me in Reno to see the house, and she immediately approved of it for our family.

Reno is in the high desert of northern Nevada. It is located
within a narrow valley, with a mix of businesses and agricul-
ture, and only a forty-five-minute drive to Lake Tahoe and two

hours to Sacramento. Once the house was purchased, I drove up from Las Vegas and placed our first fixture into the home: a Little Tikes Treehouse in Laura's bedroom. We moved in during the summer of 1984 and began an enjoyable two years in a new place that felt like home.

After we were living there for a few months, we decided to hire a landscaping company to add a lawn and double-faced fence around the property. I had quietly arranged to surprise Lillie with the installation to be done while she was visiting with her sister Sherry in Denver. When Lillie returned to Reno, she was very happy to see the house now in its finished form.

I decided to practice law on my own in Reno and sublet office space with three other attorneys in an office near downtown on Lander Street. I didn't have much of a client base, and much of my new practice was based on lawyer referrals from the State Bar of Nevada. I did enjoy working with a start-up charter airline known as Comstock Airlines on a stock/fee basis. I assisted the staff as outside counsel in their efforts to establish proposed travel routes, create a reservation system, and apply with the airport authority to seek future gate assignments and airport counter space for passenger check-in and aircraft acquisition.

Comstock was negotiating the lease of an older Lockheed Electra, which was a four-propeller/engine plane. The purpose of the lease was to engage in junket operations to fly in passengers from Minneapolis and entice them with casino attractions and promotions to be provided by the local casinos in South Lake Tahoe.

I worked closely with the airline company president, and I enjoyed the new career experience. Unfortunately, we were in a bidding war on the aircraft lease with Caesars Tahoe Hotel and Casino. When Caesars Tahoe won the bid, the employees of Comstock Airlines voted out its company president, and I left as well.

Sadly, the Lockheed Electra leased by Caesars had a problem upon its departure from the Reno airport to return passengers to Minneapolis after their junket trip to Caesars Tahoe. An aircraft technician reportedly failed to secure a service flap on the plane. Upon takeoff from Reno, the plane began to vibrate, and as a result, the pilot cut back on power and the plane stalled, then crashed south of the airport near South Virginia Street. About eighty passengers perished, though one person miraculously survived with barely a scratch. We heard the sound of the double explosion from our house that evening. When I learned of what had happened and that the plane was the same aircraft we had been bidding on at Comstock, my heart began to pound heavily. It wasn't until the next day that we discovered the full extent of the crash and the tragic loss of life.

I continued with my legal practice for a couple of years, but there was no referral base to assist in promoting my legal services. Fortunately, we still had our casino investment in Las Vegas to help support us. It was also during this time that I applied for another gaming license, which required more investigation and hearings.

An agent from the Nevada Gaming Control Board made an appointment to interview me at my office. The interviews are usually recorded by the agent. He asked me if I knew or recognized some individuals with ethnic-sounding names who lived in Kansas City, Philadelphia, and other Midwest and East Coast locations. I answered honestly that their names were not familiar to me.

"Tell me about your uncle Nathan," he then said.

"What do you want to know?" I asked.

"What does he do for a living?"

I was suspicious of his line of questioning but said the only thing I knew for sure. "Uncle Nate assists in the management and operation of the family bakery in upstate New York. Is there something else I should know?"

He shook his head. In later years, family circles confirmed that my uncle Nate was a well-known bookmaker doing business with the S&G Syndicate on Miami Beach, but I honestly didn't know that at the time. Uncle Nate was always very private, and I didn't know much about him or have the occasion to spend any significant time with him.

The questions continued. "When was the last time you spoke with your brother, Steven?"

"I spoke to him about a month ago."

"Do you know that you engaged in a conversation with someone who has a warrant out for his arrest?" the agent asked.

I had no idea that Steven was wanted for any crime—in this case, it turned out to be the passing of bad checks, also known as issuing checks with insufficient funds. When the interview concluded, I walked quickly to a pay phone outside a nearby convenience store. I asked Steve why he didn't tell me that he was in trouble with the law. He didn't really have a response. Maybe he thought there was no need for me to know about his situation.

One matter did come up in the interview with the agent that I needed legal counsel to assist me with. Before leaving my law office, the agent asked me to allow him to review my client files. I explained to him that my client files were confidential and privileged. He responded that I waived all my privileges as a necessary part of the gaming investigatory process. I agreed that I had waived *my* privileges but not my clients' privileges, which were protected under the attorney-client privilege.

As the agent left, he said he would report back to his supervisors that I was not cooperative and he would recommend denial of my license application. The agent's position was unreasonable, and he probably was not well versed in the meaning behind a confidential attorney-client privilege. I felt sure that I wasn't the first attorney ever to apply for a Nevada gaming license and assumed that if the demand was made to another attorney, the same situation might occur. Through some negotiations we reached an agreement that allowed the agent to look at the name tabs on my client files, but not to review the information or contents of those files. In a couple of months, I was granted another Nevada gaming license, which placed my casino investment into a solely owned corporation.

After two years of living in Reno, we realized the city didn't give us everything we were hoping for in a place to raise a family. While Reno was close to Sacramento and just a one-hour flight from my family in Las Vegas, we wanted to look toward the future. My legal practice in Reno was not strong because we did not know many people in the community, and my father's connections were centered in Las Vegas. Lillie was then pregnant with our second child, David, so we had a growing family to consider. Lillie expressed interest in moving back to Sacramento, but I preferred returning to Florida, where we had both grown up.

The advantages were that I was already a licensed attorney in Florida and that Lillie's family was there for us to share our growing family with. I was also not excited about the thought of studying for and taking a third bar exam, the California Bar, as it is one of the most difficult bar exams to pass in the country. We finally decided to return home to South Florida.

David was born in Reno in the summer of 1986 as we were preparing to move. We sold our home in Reno quickly; however, we still needed to hold a Jewish ceremonial bris for our son before moving. Friends and family joined us at our house in Reno for the occasion. My mother and her husband, Kap, flew in from Las Vegas, as did my sister, my father, and his wife, Zola. Steve arrived from Los Angeles, and we gave him the honor of being the godfather to David.

This was one of the few times in my life that I recall all five members of my family being in the same place at the same time. It was exciting to share a special family occasion with everyone, though it was clear they were just tolerating each other for the event. My mother noticed later that she was missing twenty dollars from her purse. She insinuated that Steve had not changed. Everyone returned home (Steve still under a Nevada arrest warrant), and we then moved to Florida when David was five weeks old.

CHAPTER 14

Family Life in Boca Raton

While Lillie and I had grown up in Highland Lakes and North Miami Beach in Dade County, now known as Miami-Dade County, we decided that we wanted to experience living in a new community. We had heard that Boca Raton was a good place for raising a family and would offer us more of the traditional Jewish community that we'd missed in Reno. We found a beautiful neighborhood with tree-lined streets known as Millpond. The house was a four-bedroom, two-and-a-half-bath, single-family residence with a backyard swimming pool. There were many young families in the community with children. This became our home for the next eighteen years.

On move-in day, our next-door neighbor Maddi Sackel came over to introduce herself and her family. She had two young girls, and her husband, Stephen, was a physician. We felt so warmly welcomed by her—she even brought us a cheesecake from a local pastry shop as a welcoming gesture. We also met other families on our street and in the community, and it all seemed right.

We explored the community for grocery shopping, clothing needs, and school options for Laura, who was three years old. There were parks and children's gymnastics studios, and the beach was just a ten-minute car ride from our house. Laura also began swimming lessons in Boca Raton that year. We selected a private school for her to begin pre-K classes, then known as Boca Raton Academy, which was not more than five minutes from our home. She began making many friends and some remain her closest friends and soulmates to this day.

In the area, I had a somewhat-distant relative, and my uncle Iggy arranged for us to meet. His name was Sid Krutick, and the best that I can recollect, he was my mother's first cousin. Sid and his wife, Esther, were senior citizens who lived in nearby Delray Beach in the Kings Point senior community. Sid was a retired pharmacist, spoke with a gravelly voice, and walked slowly with the use of a cane.

Sometime after settling in, Sid asked me to join him to see a chiropractor in Delray Beach named Andre Fladell. I explained to Sid that I was feeling fine and didn't need to see a chiropractor. He insisted that we meet with his chiropractor, so we did.

Sid was president of the Kings Point Democratic Club, which was one of many South Florida political organizations that had organized voting blocs to assist in determining which candidates would succeed in their political campaigns and what community issues would receive the voting support of these high-turnout communities. So, how does a chiropractor fit into this story? When I walked into Dr. Fladell's chiropractic office in Delray Beach with Sid, the doctor shook my hand and asked, "Are you trying to take away my power?" I was initially clueless.

I then realized that he stated this in jest and as an introduction to who he was. It turned out that Dr. Andre Fladell was a political power broker. He had created an organization known

as the South County Political Cooperative. Dr. Fladell and invited members worked together to promote a high voter turn-
out in the senior citizen communities. Large voting blocs were
managed by the cooperative in the senior citizen precincts so
that preferred candidates would be elected to office and voter
support or opposition to new laws or ordinances that affected
the community would be properly organized. Knowing Andre
and having his support as a "kingmaker" would most likely determine your political future in those days.

As I was a young attorney and family man trying to become established in his new surroundings, Sid wanted to get
me involved in the Palm Beach County community and asked
Andre for his assistance. Within a year, I became chairman of
the Transportation Committee of the South County Political
Cooperative, overseeing such issues as the possible exten-
sion of the Sawgrass Expressway from Broward County into
western Palm Beach County, and the creation and future operations of a commuter rail service that would be known as
Tri-Rail.

Sid also introduced me to some of the county commissioners for Palm Beach County, and I received my first gov-
ernmental board appointment to the Palm Beach County
Comprehensive Planning Committee for planning and zoning issues. I joined various political organizations and began
making a good name for myself in organizing and conducting
grassroots efforts for the community. I very much enjoyed this
new, thought-provoking, and unexpected involvement in the
local political scene.

As if I didn't have enough on my hands with my new work
in local politics and managing our casino investment in Las
Vegas, I also decided to open a private legal practice in Boca
Raton. I began representing clients in real estate, estate planning, joint ventures, and business law matters. I also sought
out gaming law matters when such opportunities arose. I

maintained both my Nevada and Florida Bar licenses, as I wanted to be able to also assist my father and family in Nevada if needed.

My father was always looking for business opportunities, and during the late 1980s he was introduced to a gentleman who was operating the Jaragua Hotel and Casino in Santo Domingo, Dominican Republic. The owner expressed an interest in purchasing gaming equipment for his casino. On behalf of my father, I met with this gentleman in Fort Lauderdale to discuss the equipment and was invited to visit the Jaragua casino. I asked the prospective purchaser when he had time for my visit, thinking I would make travel arrangements from Miami International Airport. Surprisingly, he asked if I could leave the next day and meet him at Fort Lauderdale Executive Airport.

I packed a small suitcase and arrived at the airport to find that the owner was a pilot with a private Citation jet, and that he and his copilot would take me with his colleagues to Santo Domingo. This was the first time I had ever flown on a private plane. We began our journey over the aqua waters of the Caribbean Basin, traversing through the Bahamian Archipelago and then crossing over the shores of Hispaniola. I sat in the flight deck as we began our descent into the lush green and narrow valleys of the Dominican Republic. When we deplaned in Santo Domingo, we were quickly escorted around the customs area, as would a VIP, to a waiting vehicle.

I spent two days visiting and touring the gaming property, and my father sold the casino several slot machines, coin-flip games known as Flip-It, and some casino signage by verbal agreement. The terms were $30,000 plus cost of shipment, and as my father would often do, the agreement was finalized by a virtual handshake and a matter of contractual trust. It was an interesting and different travel and business experience for me, and I was glad to assist my father in advancing his business opportunities and sales in the Caribbean. I started to feel like I could be of some importance to him in business.

But, as it turned out, my father never received payment for the shipped goods, and it would be extremely difficult to collect the debt owed to him as his equipment was now off-shore and the legal system would favor local businessmen. The casino operator was well aware of this and probably had no intention of ever paying for the merchandise. The only consolation was that amazing travel and aviation experience for me.

When I was home, I continued to engage in political activities in Palm Beach County, attending countless meetings of the local Democratic clubs and nonpartisan organizations such as the Voters Coalition. I was gaining a good and strong political following, and I was often told that I maintained such integrity, an attractive asset for someone involved in politics.

Lillie and I worked hard at home, raising our two children in a loving and caring household. We took wonderful trips to the nearby zoos, Butterfly World, and the Florida Keys, and each October spent special time at my mother and Kap's time-share unit on the beaches of Sanibel Island. We enjoyed taking our children snow skiing in California or Colorado during their school winter break, and in the summer, we went to our favorite hideaway at the Balsams in Dixville Notch, northern New Hampshire.

We must have spent at least ten summer vacations at the Balsams, an all-inclusive resort that originally opened in the 1860s. It offered wonderful lodging accommodations with fine dining, a children's camp program, activities like movies and bingo on rainy days, and the most beautiful hiking trails through the woods and around the lakes and ponds of the area. We often saw moose and some deer, and on one occasion, a brown bear was spotted while we were out walking a trail. The Balsams was a place where we, as a family, could recharge and get away from the stress and responsibilities that we dealt with during the year at home.

On one of our summer vacation trips to New England in the early 1990s, we decided to drive up the East Coast. At the same time, my father had an opportunity to sell gaming equipment to a tribal casino on the sovereign lands of the Crow Nation in Montana. There were often problematic legal disputes between the state and the tribe regarding permitted gaming activities. While the Supreme Court had ruled that federally recognized tribes could engage in gaming activities on reservation land, some of the states had initially resisted this activity within their borders. Unfortunately, my father wound up in the crosshairs of one of these legal disputes.

My father did not correctly complete and submit the regulatory documentation to support the sale and shipment of gaming equipment into Montana. It may have been as simple a matter as my father placing the name of his company, Games of Nevada, on the regulatory submission requesting the name of the game manufacturer, which was actually Bally. However, Montana used this innocently made mistake to punish my father and a colleague and make an example out of them, just another escalation in the legal battle and tensions between Montana gaming and tribal gaming authorities. My father was notified that he was being charged with felony counts against him for the illegal shipment of gaming equipment into Montana.

My father was shaken, as he knew that the mere placement of criminal charges against him would cause regulatory scrutiny and licensing concern over his gaming licenses in Nevada. His livelihood depended on his gaming licenses being maintained in good standing. So I searched for a criminal attorney in Helena, Montana, to review the case and represent my father.

While I was on my family summer trip in New Hampshire, my father called to say that the court had scheduled a bench trial date for his case in Helena—in three days. I needed to get my family home, pick up a suit, and attend the court appearances. We immediately left New Hampshire, Lillie and I taking turns driving at a hectic pace to make it home in two days. I packed a suitcase and got dropped off at the Fort Lauderdale airport within three hours of getting back. After two layovers, I met my father in Helena that evening with the trial commencing the following morning.

For the next two days I watched the case presented by Montana's prosecutors and the defenses raised by my father's counsel, Mark Yeshe. At the end of the trial but before judgment was pronounced, the prosecution approached the defense counsel and offered my father a plea arrangement to accept a misdemeanor charge rather than face the prospect of a possible felony conviction. Although on the surface this sounds reasonable from a criminal law perspective, even a mere misdemeanor charge related to gaming could lead to devastating results to your gaming licenses, which were granted as a privilege, and not a right, by the gaming regulatory body.

My father chose not to accept the plea bargain and waited for the judge to enter judgment on the felony charges at a hearing set for the following day. It was the longest night I ever spent, with heavy anguish apparent on my father's face over the hours. It felt like his whole life was balancing on the edge of a cliff.

The next morning, the judge recited the facts of the case and then pronounced his judgment on the felony charge against my father: "Not guilty!" We were so relieved. Some months later, when my father appeared before the Nevada Gaming Control Board on a new licensing matter, he was questioned by then member and former FBI agent Bobby Siller. Mr. Siller questioned my father about the court case that had transpired in Montana. My father responded, "Mr. Siller, I was found innocent." Mr. Siller then responded to my father, "No, you were found not guilty." Despite the semantics, my father's gaming licenses remained intact and in good standing.

I became more involved in political activities on the national level and began working with the Clinton/Gore presidential campaign in South Florida. I gave speeches on their behalf in South Florida, had the opportunity to meet with Al Gore when he descended from the steps of Air Force Two at the Boca Raton Airport, and met with President Clinton during the State Democratic Party Convention in Orlando. We met on the day that impeachment proceedings were announced relating to his interactions with White House intern Monica Lewinsky. These were exciting times for me.

One day, I returned to my law office in Boca Raton and received a call from my father relating to my brother, Steven. He asked me to come to Las Vegas immediately. Steve had incredible talents in sales and marketing. He began his sales career by selling dictionaries door-to-door with the tactic of placing his foot on the doorjamb so that the customer couldn't quickly shut the door and end his pitch. He then worked assembling teams to sell steak knife sets and earned commissions from everyone on his team. He was capable of achieving great success. His mind was sharp, and he worked with strategy and precision in everything that he approached.

However, Steve was the product of two broken homes by the time he was thirteen years old. After his mother (my mother's sister Eleanor) died, he and his siblings were deserted by their father, so my parents adopted Steve only to divorce a few years later, resulting in a second broken home. I believe this had a great impact on his personality and stability.

When I arrived in Las Vegas, I met with my father and Steve, who had just been released on bail from the Clark County Detention Center after he, once again, was being charged with passing more bad checks. Not only did Steve pass bad checks in Clark County, but he did so throughout Nevada and in Los Angeles. He had eight felony charges brought against him. This was not his first offense, and our father was done with it.

"I'm tired of paying for attorneys to defend you in court," he said to Steve. "You should have your brother represent you."

I was shocked, and from Steve's face, I could see he felt the same. "Dad," I said, "I don't know the first thing about representing a client, not to mention my brother, in a criminal proceeding."

"Maybe this is a good time to learn," he responded. The conversation was over.

Steve was represented by a public defender in Clark County, and I handled the remaining felony charges filed in Winnemucca, Ely, Carson City, Tonopah, Reno, and Los Angeles. The public defender did not represent Steve well, and he was convicted. At the end, Judge Addeliar Guy asked my brother about his sense of the severity of his crimes. Steve responded, "Your Honor, I have not even received a traffic ticket in my life."

Judge Guy was not moved by my brother's response, sentencing him to two years in medium security in the Nevada State penal system. For the next two years, I visited Steve in prison as he was moved around to Ely, Carson City, and finally a minimum-security facility in Indian Springs. Because I was an attorney, I could visit Steve in a private room, and we could talk without guards or anyone listening. I bought him prison clothes, which consisted of a blue denim long-sleeved shirt, jeans, and sneakers. I was also permitted to pay for him to own a small TV and provided money on account to purchase cigarettes, a necessity in prison.

The inmates bartered cigarettes for whatever they needed outside of what was permitted. These visits were the first time

I had ever been inside a prison, and I will never forget seeing inmates behind bars wearing orange jumpsuits, shackled from their wrists to their ankles. The restrained inmates could not even lift a hand to their face to take a drag on their cigarettes, instead contorting their bodies in an uncomfortable maneuver to smoke.

Steve experienced many of the hardships inherent in prison life, as he was not the same person when he was released two years later. During his first year, he was able to work in the religious center because he was one of the few Jewish inmates. He assisted another inmate, the son of a rabbi, in setting up for religious services. This inmate was serving a very long sentence for killing someone and then placing the victim's severed head in a box on the doorstep of their family's home. Why my brother was placed in a medium-security prison with violent criminals just for issuing a series of bad checks is beyond my comprehension. I felt so terrible each time I concluded my allotted visiting time, knowing that Steve could not leave with me.

After serving his first year in prison, Steve applied to be considered for parole and early release. Just prior to the Pardon Board hearing, he uttered to me, "Hope for the best but expect the worst." I was able to lobby for one of the three votes cast by the Pardon Board, but Steve's request for parole was denied. This denial meant he would face another year behind bars. In the prison vernacular, he was "dumped" by the Pardon Board.

During the last year of his sentence, I diligently worked through all the remaining charges filed against him in other jurisdictions. I explained to the prosecutors assigned to his case in each jurisdiction about who my brother was, how he was a product of two broken homes, and that he was a good person with a tendency to emotionally spiral. Though he had engaged in intentional acts leading to financial crimes, I vouched that he didn't have a physical or threatening criminal mindset. I don't know why I was so fortunate in my efforts, but I was able to get all of Steve's remaining felony counts dismissed.

I had lengthy telephone discussions with the prosecutors in each county who were assigned to my brother's criminal file. The discussions were simply about facts and history, not questioning the application of law. When speaking with the prosecutors, especially if they were also graduates of the McGeorge School of Law as I was, I'd state plainly, "Steven is a good person with a good soul. He is misguided as a result of being the product of two broken homes before he attained the age of thirteen. I ask you to take into account his childhood history when considering if he should serve additional time when he completes his current sentence."

I must have worked on these seven criminal charges for over a year and a half before I had something to report. Steve called me from prison one day, and I said, "Steve, I have some good news to share with you. I have been able to have all the remaining felony counts from the various counties dropped against you. You will not be facing any additional prosecution when you are released from your current sentence."

With utter joy in his voice on the other end of the line, he said, "Glenn, you hit a home run!"

Once he finished his prison sentence, he was released on Fremont Street in downtown Las Vegas and given a twenty-dollar bill. He was now an ex-felon with no job and no home to go to. Claudia agreed to let him stay with her in Las Vegas, and I lobbied my father to place Steve on the company payroll for temporary financial support to further justify and legally support his release on parole. This was all done with the clear understanding that Steve was not to set foot on the business premises nor be engaged in any business matters of the company. My father was concerned about his gaming licenses and about Steve causing any additional problems for him and the family.

Steve lived with Claudia for a while until he was able to get an apartment of his own. His next step was addressing his dental needs—he was missing many teeth when he was released. The extractions had not been health-related, though. There was apparently a practice in the prison system where the dentist received some type of premium for the number of teeth he extracted.

I would see Steve occasionally in Las Vegas after his release, but he never was the same person. He would tell me that he just didn't have the energy to jump-start his life again after the ordeal of prison. About two years after his release, I received a call from my sister. Steve had attempted to take his own life and was in the hospital. I spoke with my father, whose concern about the severity of the attempt was clear. He hoped we would not be soon attending a funeral. After his release from the hospital, Steve made a second attempt to take his own life and tragically succeeded. Steve was fifty years old. I was numb, though not shocked, when I learned of his death. He was in an emotional downward spiral, had a strong intention to end his life, and accomplished doing so.

My father and I were emotionally resigned to the fact that Steve had led a troubled life, though he had tried to live a good and respectable one to the best of his ability. Steve carried a small picture of our father in his wallet as a person he loved and looked up to as a guiding force in his life. Claudia was upset with members of our family who had loaned Steve money to pursue a business opportunity. She knew Steve's personality and tendencies much better than we did, since he had lived with her following his prison release, and she thought giving him money was akin to offering cocaine to a drug addict. We learned later that Steve had gambled away the money that was loaned to him. We had a small family gathering in Claudia's living room to express our thoughts and memories of Steve, but there was no formal memorial service. Steve had been in and out of my life so many times that his passing felt surreal. He was my big brother and cheerleader. I miss him dearly to this day.

Back in Florida, I returned to my life, which was as normal as it could be. My wife and family were my bedrock. I continued with my political activities and modest legal practice and helped my father when I could. One day, he asked me if I would travel to Port-au-Prince, Haiti, on a day trip to meet with an attorney who represented some individual or company. I didn't know the specifics, but I always tried to be helpful to him. While en route, I developed some kind of stomach virus that made me sick and weak. I arrived in Port-au-Prince and was met by a driver, but I was extremely ill. I lay back in the reclined passenger seat while the driver navigated through the downtown area.

I was able to regain enough energy to leave the car and walk up to the attorney's office. I was handed an envelope. Done with my duty, I asked to be taken back to the airport to go home. I was clearly ill, and the attorney suggested I first see a local doctor, but I had read about the very poor health-care system in Haiti and the large number of patients who experienced renal failure after receiving routine medical treatments. I declined the offer and returned to the airport.

While I was hoping to purchase a ticket to board a flight to Miami, I was told the flight was sold out. I was informed that the next flight would be in an hour departing for JFK airport in New York City. I asked for a ticket to travel to New York and figured I would find an easier way home from there. While I was walking across the tarmac toward the flight leaving for New York, an airline agent ran up, letting me know that there was now one open seat in first class on the flight to Miami. I gratefully flew home. I honestly didn't know what was in the envelope, but I forwarded it to my father in Las Vegas. I had no reason to believe that I was doing anything more than forwarding a payment to my father.

On another occasion, my father wanted to explore the manufacture of gaming equipment on the island of Jamaica. Jamaica was an up-and-coming gaming jurisdiction served by large corporations such as IGT and a gaming division of Carnival Cruise Line. The idea was to have a joint venture with a Jamaican appliance company, finalizing assembly for slot machines manufactured in South Korea. With the three companies working together, they could avoid the 104 percent import duty that would otherwise be assessed upon the imported finished product.

While I had personal reservations about the lack of quality in the South Korean gaming devices, we went forward with the opportunity. I attended meetings in Kingston with the Jamaican trade ministry, JAMPRO, and the manufacturing facility. On one trip, I was staying at the downtown Wyndham Hotel in Kingston and set my alarm clock to wake me up at 7:00 the next morning. I was awakened instead at 5:00 by the sound of gunshots outside. I looked out my window to see a person lying in the street and someone kicking their motionless body. I was shocked, though I later learned this kind of scene may have been more common in that area than I would have otherwise believed. I couldn't wait to get back home.

After a day of touring the facility, the Jamaican company owner wanted to drive me and another colleague over the mountains north of Kingston to Ocho Rios on a day trip. The owner had a heavy foot on and off the car accelerator, which made my back-seat journey uncomfortable. We reached the top of the mountain pass between Kingston and Ocho Rios just after a rainstorm had passed. The roads were slick, and within seconds, our car went out of control, spinning around many times and ultimately stopping just at the edge of the cliff.

I felt that if I even sneezed or coughed, it would be enough to cause us to drop off the cliff. I was thankful that afterward we were stuck behind a very slow truck on a single-lane road, and I began to breathe again.

On the day that I was scheduled to depart for Miami, heavy rains descended upon Jamaica. The streets were heavily flooded, but the taxi was able to somehow make it to the airport terminal. As I checked in and walked to the general departure lounge, the water level began to rise, creeping into the terminal floor and, ultimately, people had to stand on the airport lounge chairs to get out of the water. Workers opened utility panels on the floor to drain the flooded terminal. As the floodwater began to recede through the floor panels, hundreds—if not thousands—of cockroaches spewed up and into the terminal. All of us waiting passengers continued to stand on our seats until the unwelcome visitors had been cleared out of the terminal. I finally boarded my flight, taking off into the heavy rainstorm, but the skilled pilot got us home safely.

CHAPTER 15

Political Campaign for the Florida House of Representatives

In the fall of 1995, I was invited to breakfast in Boca Raton by a political lobbyist, Meril Stumberger, who represented real estate developers for land use and zoning matters. There were many changes to the political landscape in Palm Beach County as our congressman, Harry Johnston, announced his plans to retire at the end of his term. Subsequent to Johnston's announcement, Senator Robert Wexler declared his intention to run for the congressional seat while Representative Ron Klein sought the resulting open Senate seat.

These ladder-climbing political events resulted in an open seat in District 89 of the Florida House of Representatives. District 89, which has since been redistricted, covered a large area of southern Palm Beach County that included Central and West Boca Raton and West Delray Beach. The voters in this district were primarily retirees and senior citizens, mostly lifelong Democrats, and a good percentage of the voters were Jewish. Most of these voters had also relocated to South Florida from the New York / New Jersey area.

Meril was a skilled and influential lobbyist, someone who would just come out and say what was on her mind. We sat down for breakfast together at TooJay's Deli in Boca Raton and began chatting. We knew of each other but didn't really know much about each other's lives and families. Maybe five minutes into the discussion, Meril came straight out and asked me if I would be interested in running for public office, specifically for the open House seat. I had never considered running for office and had always been content supporting candidates or working on community issues on a grassroots level.

I told her I was honored to be considered but wanted to run the thought by my wife before making any commitments. While Lillie shared my initial surprise, she was very supportive of the idea. Later in the day I informed Meril that I wanted to pursue the opportunity if it came with her political support and assistance. What followed was not the easy path that I had been led to believe I would be heading down. I truly did not know what it was like to be the focus of a political campaign or how it would overtake my day-to-day life.

Four candidates chose to run for this open seat, including myself. There was Scott Brenner, a commercial real estate broker with strong ties to the property developers in Broward and Palm Beach Counties. Barry Silver was an attorney and considered to be a far-left-of-center candidate who was quite flamboyant and known to represent high-profile clients to push social causes and gain public visibility and notoriety. His father was also a well-known rabbi in Delray Beach with a thirty-year congregational following. Guarina Klein was an educator who possibly hoped to capitalize on having the same last name as the departing state House member for the district. Then there was me.

It was a grueling eleven-month campaign composed of countless public appearances and speeches before memberships of the various Democratic clubs, meetings with political officials and lobbying groups, fundraising events, team strategy meetings, trips to Tallahassee to meet with then-Governor Lawton Chiles, live political debates and presentations on local television networks, and studying the important issues every day so that I would always know what was being asked and how to intelligently respond to the questions posed.

I clipped articles from the local newspapers each day related to political and social issues of interest in the community. I then organized these articles in separate manila file folders with tab headings such as crime, insurance, environmental issues, education, and other politically relevant categories. I reviewed each article and prepared a summary of each on a legal pad, studying the summaries every day of the campaign. I never wanted to be caught off guard when being asked questions in a public forum, and I became known as a candidate who had a deep understanding of the issues that were affecting the community.

My mother and I walked through the senior communities at night and handed out bags of cookies to the residents as they entered the movie theater in their complex. We went door-to-door in Century Village in Boca Raton and placed campaign hangers with my name, picture, and election information on the doors of each residence late at night. My dear friend Sherri Rothberg developed campaign marketing themes for me to apply to T-shirts and bumper stickers. One marketing effort targeted the senior citizens active in weekly bowling leagues. More cookies were wrapped in wax paper and placed in brown bags with the slogan on the bag stating: "Be a Good Cookie! Vote for Glenn Wichinsky." I personally distributed these bags of cookies every week to the senior citizens playing their leagues at the local bowling alley.

Finally, Sherri came up with the idea that we should target the snowbird voting bloc, many of whom spent summers in the Catskill Mountains, where I was born and raised. Sherri created a political advertisement and placed it in the local newspaper in the Catskills. It had my picture and election information along with the slogan: "Support a Mountain Boy! Vote for Glenn Wichinsky." I also did campaign walks through the bungalow colonies of the Catskill region. My uncle Iggy, a snowbird himself, introduced me to other residents. Many of the voters would not return to South Florida before the first primary to be held in early September, so we promoted absentee voter registration to support our campaign effort.

Meanwhile, one of my opponents, Mr. Silver, was jumping up and down on a trampoline near a busy intersection of Delray Beach to draw an audience, throwing Frisbees to supporters, and singing in a shopping center with his mother accompanying him on keyboard. We agreed on the issues, but we differed greatly in style.

Raising campaign funds is a daily and arduous task that every candidate for public office faces. Even elected public officials need to prepare for their reelection bid from the first day they are sworn in to office. Large sums of money were coming into the Brenner campaign from the local developers, while the remaining candidates, including myself, took a grassroots approach and loaned personal funds to our campaigns. I had considered reaching out to the gaming industry for political contributions and support, but in 1995 the issue of legalized gambling in Florida had not yet matured and voters were generally split on the issue. I chose not to accept campaign contributions from the gaming industry as a result. All campaign contributions I received were reported to the Supervisor of Elections office and made public.

In one public candidate's forum, one of my opponent's supporters asked me why I was accepting campaign contributions from the gaming industry. He noted that I had reported two campaign contributions that came from addresses in Las Vegas. I smiled and responded that the Las Vegas contributions were from my own father and mother.

After many months of nonstop campaigning and losing over twenty pounds on my already slight physical frame, we were finally nearing the first primary in early September. I was fortunate to gain the endorsements of all three major newspapers, the *Sun Sentinel*, *The Palm Beach Post*, and the *Boca Raton News*, in addition to many industry groups. When Election Day arrived, I was standing at the polling station for Century Village, shaking hands and distributing voter recommendation pamphlets known as palm cards. These were printed by different organizations or interest groups with a listing of their candidate or issue recommendations for voters to consider before casting their votes.

After a full day campaigning at the polls with my team and supporters, I drove home to awaiting family and friends for the early election results to be released. By ten o'clock that evening, the results of the District 89 House race showed that Barry Silver had received the most votes at approximately 47 percent but, as no Republican candidates had filed in the race, it was less than the 50 percent needed to clinch the race and the seat. I came in second place with a respectable 30 percent, though there was still a significant gap for me to gain in the second primary. Mr. Silver and I would face each other in a runoff election in thirty days. There was momentary happiness and relief that the first primary was over. I took a deep breath and relaxed for that one evening. The next morning, we got up and restarted campaigning.

My team helped me place new campaign signs throughout the district. There were more speeches, campaign stops, and door-to-door campaigning in the district to gain the necessary support from any remaining undecided voters. Mr. Silver and

I ran clean campaigns without directing any attacks against each other. We agreed on all the issues, but many viewed me as more moderate and willing to work with those on the other side of the aisle.

It was important to gain as many of the votes as possible that had been cast for Mr. Brenner and Ms. Klein during the first primary, and it was just as important to gain the endorsement of any senior voting bloc that may have endorsed one of them. The Century Village Democratic Club was a prominent voting bloc representing hundreds of Democratic senior voters in Boca Raton. Their president was a woman named Ronnie Loeb. While I got along well with most people in political circles, for some reason Mrs. Loeb and I never hit it off. I believe her dislike for me was not personal but more directed at some of my political supporters whom she just didn't like. She would refer to them as "my handlers." Despite this, I spoke with her and kindly requested the endorsement of her club. Instead, she lobbied her board of directors to endorse Mr. Silver, whom she was not very fond of either. I was shocked and dismayed, as her efforts alone could determine the outcome of my race.

You might think that a candidate can control everything that transpires during a well-managed political campaign, but nothing could be further from the truth. While you can monitor what you say, what you place in print, and how you manage your supporters, there are always independent efforts by third parties that also influence your campaign.

Toward the end of the second primary campaign, a letter was circulated to the media on shocking-pink paper stock that blasted Mr. Silver for some alleged conduct that did not place him in a good moral light. The letter then continued, describing me as a good and decent person and family man, and a candidate who should be supported. I was approached by the media and asked why I would slam my opponent with unsubstantiated allegations at the last moment of the campaign. I responded that it didn't come from me. I assumed it was written and circulated by someone associated with one of the former candidates who was disgruntled that their candidate did not make it to the second primary. I immediately called Mr. Silver.

"Barry, there is a letter being circulated today that I just became aware of after questions from the news media. The letter does not paint you in a good light, and I want you to know that it was not developed or circulated by me or my campaign."

After a slight pause, Barry responded, "Glenn, I know who you are, and I appreciate you letting me know. I accept what you are telling me."

In early October, the second primary was held. I gave the campaign effort every ounce of thought and energy that I could invest. My wife and children were fully supportive, and we worked to the last minute of the campaign.

Many factions were assembling at Century Village when the polls opened at seven o'clock in the morning on Election Day. Different interests distributed their palm cards seeking to influence the voters as they walked into the polling station. Mrs. Loeb's club had printed dark yellow palm cards with Mr. Silver's name recommended for the state House seat. Sometime around ten o'clock that morning, a commotion erupted when Mrs. Loeb found there were other palm cards similar to hers, also with the same organizational heading "Villagers for Democrats," but these cards had my name as their recommended candidate instead of Mr. Silver.

Arguments ensued and I was approached by the media for an explanation. I produced five different palm cards that were circulating from different organizations and said I understood these activities were not generally regulated. Finger-pointing was going on, but I stayed out of the fray. I later learned that one of my supporters had been to a printshop in Boca Raton and noticed that the printer was printing the palm cards for

Century Village. He took a sample and had a duplicate with my name prepared by another printer using the same color paper stock and font size. Politics, in general, is not recognized as an activity of high ethics and morals. It is a very serious game played by those who want power and by the few of us who just want to do good for the betterment of our community.

When the polls closed, I received a call from the governor's office wishing me well and letting me know that I would hear from them depending on the outcome of the race. Some people were asking me about how I would staff the Tallahassee offices, but I felt these discussions were premature. When the polling results began to come in, it became clear that while I had run a very strong race and one that I would forever be proud of, I would not achieve my goal. Barry Silver secured 58 percent of the final vote as compared with my showing at 42 percent. He became the new state representative for District 89, and I began to take some time for myself while falling into depression.

My father called me after the race. "I thought you were going to beat this guy," he said. My father had financially contributed to my political campaign but never attempted to interfere with or object to my passionate pursuit of becoming an elected official. I believe he had some faith that with all the energies I had invested in the race and the positive publicity and major endorsements I had received that I was going to succeed. He was as disappointed in the result as I was. In hindsight, my father was never really impressed with actors or politicians, so his response should not have been a surprise to me.

My son, David, nine years old at the time, was kinder and more sensitive when he offered some emotional support to me. "Maybe we should have handed out more cookies during the campaign. Then you could have won the election," he said. I smiled and hugged him for his innocent advice.

As much as I coached myself each day of the eleven-month

campaign to just do my best and knew that the outcome was not assured, I felt lost when the finality became a reality. I was approached by a well-meaning voter the day after the campaign had ended who asked me, "How does it feel to be out of politics?" I didn't consider that I was out of politics, but his statement delivered a hurtful emotional sting. In addition, I had allowed my solo law practice to decline during the long campaign and wasn't sure what I was going to do to resurrect it or if this was even what I wanted to pursue again. I would be offered the opportunity to face off against Mr. Silver two years later at the end of his first term, but in the end I decided not to put my family through the long and combative political campaign again.

CHAPTER 16

Humanitarian Visit to Cuba

Shortly after the conclusion of the political campaign, I was contacted by the chair of a San Francisco–based nonprofit organization known as the Cuban Jewish Aid Society. The purpose of the organization was to bring religious and humanitarian aid to the Jewish population on the island of Cuba. Cuba once had a large Jewish population, but by the mid-1990s only three thousand Jewish people remained.

I was asked by the organization if I would be interested in seeking donations from my community relating to medical needs or religious items that could be assembled and shipped to the remaining synagogues in Cuba. My late mother-in-law, Hilda, was born and raised in Cuba, and having grown up in Miami, I was always interested in the country, so I offered my assistance. I obtained donations from businesses in South Florida and religious items from my synagogue.

The organization planned to personally deliver these

donated items in Cuba in December 1996. Some two weeks prior to their departure, I was again contacted by the chair and asked if I would like to travel with them to Cuba to engage in the people-to-people distribution effort. It sounded exciting to me, but I knew that American citizens were generally prohibited from visiting Cuba after the Cuban Revolution, which ended in 1959. I would be pleased to join them if their organization obtained US government approval for me to embark on this effort. About a week later, I received the required permission to travel to Cuba for three weeks on a humanitarian basis.

Since there were no direct commercial flights between the United States and Cuba, I and the twenty-five other members booked flights departing to Nassau in the Bahamas. From there, we could connect to a Cubana Airlines flight to Havana. Upon arriving at the José Martí Airport in Havana, we cleared customs and were transported to the Hotel Nacional, where we would stay for the first part of our journey.

The Hotel Nacional was one of the classic old hotel resorts in Havana and a notable location for gambling casinos, Mob-related activities, and a lifestyle of loose morality. While walking around the hotel, I noticed a room with framed pictures of famous people from the past, including Mob-related individuals from the 1950s. I immediately gained a sense of the history of this prominent resort and landmark. While in Havana, I was also able to connect with some of my mother-in-law's cousins who had remained after the revolution. I was permitted by the Cuban government to invite them to the hotel for a poolside lunch and provide them with items from the US, including some much-needed cash. Following a lunch consisting of *arroz con pollo*, the women in the group wrapped the chicken bones in napkins and took them home for making soup later. The conditions were—and remain—quite poor for many people on the island.

Our journey continued to Santiago de Cuba on an old

Russian Antonov An-24 propeller plane, which I doubt had been fully inspected in some time. Fortunately, we made it to the eastern coast of the island, with a plan to conduct the first bar mitzvah in Cuba since the Cuban Revolution. A rabbi from New Jersey who was on our trip had been remotely tutoring a young Cuban boy to become a bar mitzvah. A ceremony and reception were held at the old synagogue nearby, and congregants from nearby Guantanamo arrived on a flatbed truck. Purportedly, the president of Cuba, Fidel Castro, wanted to be present at the ceremony but was told that it was a religious ritual and that we did not want the event politicized. It was a wonderful and very memorable part of the trip.

We continued by bus for two weeks, visiting the Jewish congregants in the cities of Camaguey, Cienfuegos, and then back in Havana. This amazing experience I would equate to how participating in a Peace Corps mission must feel. We met with family members and their children who were affiliated with the local synagogues and provided the congregations with donated medical supplies to maintain and distribute to the congregants when needed. I also brought an instant camera on the trip and took countless photos of the young children. They would hold the picture in amazement as it developed in front of their eyes. We also visited some old Jewish cemeteries and sadly witnessed how the graves and markers had been desecrated, the cemeteries left in disarray.

On our return to Havana, we witnessed an exposition of Cuban military planes, helicopters, and other military vehicles in the city center in front of a building that had a depiction of the famed Cuban revolutionary Che Guevara. I was just in awe to have finally visited Cuba and engaged with the wonderful people whom I met on the island. For so many years, while growing up in South Florida, I wondered what it would be like to visit Cuba. It was a memorable and meaningful journey for me to take part in, not only helping the people who lived there but also learning a bit about my extended family history.

I called home from Cuba and let my wife know how the trip had been going.

"Your father has been calling," she said.

"Oh?"

"I told him you wouldn't be home for a few more days and asked if he wanted to leave a message. When I told him you were in Havana, he got pretty upset."

Lillie relayed that in his agitation, he blurted out to her, "Jesus Christ! Do you know what the Gaming Control Board is going to do with this?"

I personally couldn't imagine why the Gaming Control Board would have any interest or concern about me joining a humanitarian effort in another country. But I would later understand why my father was emotionally triggered and why he reacted as he did.

CHAPTER 17

Finding My Survivor Instinct

Once home, while trying to find my footing after the campaign experience, I started working with my father to develop and market a public gaming company that he and some former Bally associates had purchased a number of years before. The company was called Global Gaming Technology (formerly Gamex Industries) and had some gaming market prominence in the early days of Atlantic City.

We discussed the fact that California had just opened its tribal gaming market and several of the tribal nations were seeking to purchase used slot machines for their casinos. An opportunity presented itself for the sale of one hundred used slot machines for the Hopland Band of Pomo Indians in Northern California. The games were shipped from Las Vegas to a Sacramento warehouse for preinspection, approved, and then shipped to the Hopland Sho-Ka-Wah Casino. However, when they arrived, the tribe indicated that they would not pay for the equipment until the games were inspected and tested by an independent testing lab and certified for play at their casino.

The problem from a legal perspective was that the tribe had not adopted formal technical standards for gaming equipment to be operated at their casino and the contract clearly stated that the purchase of the games was to be accepted "as is." We were at a standstill, so I was asked to travel to the Hopland Rancheria to speak with one of their gaming commissioners about the problem. Since these were used games, I explained, there was no way that we could require the original manufacturer to submit the gaming machines to an independent test lab and assume the costs for testing and certification. It just wasn't done this way. The commissioner simply responded to me that perhaps I would like to spend the evening in their tribal prison. He then initiated a call to the tribal police.

I was shocked but stayed composed while trying to figure out what I should do. The potential breach-of-contract issue should not have escalated to the possibility of my being detained overnight in their jail. I excused myself from the meeting for a few minutes under the pretext of having to retrieve some important paperwork from my car. Instead, I quickly left the reservation.

Global Gaming Technology ultimately was paid 50 percent of the purchase price, which was essentially the cost of originally obtaining them. My father reacted to the situation with relative calm and expressed his appreciation for my efforts in attempting to resolve the matter. I continued to assist the company now and then but began to seek other business opportunities for myself.

During this same period, the events of 9/11 rocked the nation in so many ways. Just about everyone was affected by heightened emotions. And with the generalized fear about air travel, businesses were impacted in significant ways. I was still involved in the casino partnership, but the income faltered as tourists were not traveling to Las Vegas during this time. However, finance payments were due every month on new gaming equipment that I had recently installed. Our savings began to deplete, and we were getting very worried about what tomorrow would bring. Our daughter had left for college the year before, and we were still seeing our son through high school.

Lillie was depressed, facing personal challenges and contemplating career decisions of her own. Suffice it to say that I could not personally resolve the issues she was dealing with, and at the same time, I believe she had also fallen out of love with me. Upon arriving home from a West Coast business trip, Lillie simply said to me, "I want to be alone and on my own." I was deeply saddened upon learning of her decision.

We had been a part of each other's lives for close to three decades, and my family was everything to me. All I can say is that I was devastated by this for many years, both emotionally and financially, and I had a choice to make about whether to find a way to survive or not. I believe I found my strength in my children and wanted to stay healthy for them.

I decided I didn't want to face the pain and grief of my divorce every month through spousal support payments, so I offered a lump-sum settlement in my divorce. I essentially started my life over again at age fifty-one and entered a new chapter with relatively little income and no savings. Following the divorce proceedings in 2004, I mentioned to a colleague how shocked I was by everything that had transpired and how "I didn't see the train coming." He was also divorced and responded, "In my case, I was driving the locomotive."

I moved back to Las Vegas, living in hotel and motel rooms for a while as I sought something to economically sustain myself and give me some purpose in this frightening new life chapter. Our son remained at home in Florida with Lillie to complete his senior year of high school. Fortunately, a business opportunity arrived that provided some level of direction and security for me.

Jack Godfrey was our family's gaming counsel for licensing matters in Nevada, and he and his partner Frank Schreck had been formidable and highly respected attorneys in Nevada for many years. Jack had approached me and Claudia with a proposition on behalf of a client. His client owned a dormant stand-alone casino on the banks of the Colorado River in Laughlin, Nevada. The owner wanted to have the property licensed for gaming and liquor operations before the grandfathered rights to his property as a stand-alone casino terminated in December of that year.

Since Claudia and I had been investigated and licensed many times by the Nevada Gaming Control Board, we had the opportunity to submit for licensing to open and operate this gaming property before the December 31 deadline. In return, if we were successful, the owners would provide us with a two-year operating lease on the gaming location. The client would pay for all costs of investigation and licensing and do a full renovation of the property prior to opening. Claudia and I agreed to pursue the opportunity.

With the legal and regulatory assistance of Jack and Frank, we were successful in obtaining the required gaming licenses and conducting a soft opening of the Regency Casino before the deadline. But there was still work to do to fully reopen the casino.

Within three months, Claudia and I oversaw the renovation and opened the casino with sixty-five employees. We established bar operations on both levels of the casino; sublet the restaurant operations to a couple who operated a restaurant in nearby Bullhead City, Arizona; placed seventy-five gaming machines that were purchased on credit from our father; set up security and cage operations; and opened it all to the public. During the three-month preoperating period, I was living in a fifteen-dollar-per-night room at the Edgewater Hotel, right next door to the casino.

Once the casino was open, my day would begin at four o'clock in the morning, when I supervised the drop procedures for emptying the coins of each machine, which were then counted and verified in the casino cage by the cage supervisor. It took some time to complete, but I made sure we were ready to open the casino doors by 7:00 each morning. If there was time, I traveled across the nearby bridge to Bullhead City, where I enjoyed a quiet and smoke-free breakfast at the Black Bear Diner. Upon returning to the casino, I oversaw daily operations until 11:00 p.m. It was like *Groundhog Day* set in a casino, each day a repeat of the prior one. It felt unreal. I was living in a very basic hotel room in a town of only 9,500 residents when, just the year before, I was living in my home in Boca Raton with my family, nearby friends, and familiar surroundings. My solace was being able to drive four hours to Los Angeles on some weekends so I could visit Laura, who was then attending the University of Southern California.

At times I walked the boardwalk behind the casino, which ran along the banks of the Colorado River, wondering where life might take me while continuing to despair about all that I had lost. The boardwalk led to a sand bluff alongside the river, where I sat and took in the beautiful scenery of the mountains on the Arizona side. While I could appreciate the amazing desert landscape in front of me, I could not take my mind from where I was now living without my home, family, and friends. I wondered if there was a life to enjoy after such great loss. The fact that I had practically lost all that I had worked for was a constant drumbeat in my mind.

There were warning signs posted about the strong currents and undertows along the banks of the Colorado River, and I would look at those signs, occasionally pondering whether it was all worth it. However, I didn't want to cause more harm and pain to my parents after my brother took his life, and I wanted to stay as strong and healthy as I could for my children.

Then I met Melissa, a recent hire in the casino who was also lost in her own life. One day, she approached the cage manager of the casino, Carol, and asked if she could keep some of her earnings in safekeeping at the casino as she was having some type of domestic dispute with her husband, from whom she was trying to separate. Carol asked if I would speak with her to see how we might be helpful to her. I made an appointment to meet with her the next day.

She came into the meeting distressed over some incident with her husband. I tried to comfort her, letting her know that we were all supportive of her personal needs and well-being. As I was leaving for Florida the next day to visit my son, I gave Melissa my personal phone number and asked her to call if I could assist her in any way while out of town.

Over time, we developed a deep friendship and later a romantic relationship while being discreet at the casino and in our small town of a few thousand people. We arrived at and left the casino separately out of the front and back doors, and if we decided to see a movie together in town, we would enter the theater one at a time. This routine continued for close to a year before my sister became aware of the relationship. Claudia was upset and seemed intent to see it quickly end. I don't know if she acted negatively toward Melissa at first because she thought she was protecting me or for some reason related to my dating an employee, but after the situation became public, Melissa resigned from her casino position. We continued our relationship, though, and her love, caring, and support made me feel alive again.

Our casino operations ended after one year, when the property owners decided to apply for their own gaming licenses. The transfer of operations and ownership was not a smooth one, as the owners ordered that Claudia and I shut down the operations and terminate the employment of all the personnel. We tried to reason with the property owners about the impact this would have on the sixty-five employees who depended on their jobs and weekly paychecks, but our expressed concerns were ignored.

It was a sad ending to what we had created at the Regency Casino. The casino reopened sometime later after undergoing additional renovations. Claudia and I received a one-year buy-out on the lease and then said goodbye to our friends and colleagues in Laughlin.

I was fortunate that my quest for survival led me to stepping stones for optimism and growth in my personal and professional life. I moved back to Las Vegas, as did Melissa. Our relationship continued for three more years. It sadly ended, mainly because I was not emotionally or financially prepared to start a new married life with her so soon after the end of my twenty-eight-year marriage.

In Las Vegas, some business and investment people who were operating a San Diego–based gaming development company called VirtGame came knocking. VirtGame was developing server-based gaming and sports-betting kiosks; their investors were looking for a new president to work with their chief executive officer. I interviewed and was hired for the Las Vegas–based position. The company had limited public funding, and while it developed interesting products, we had to either seek a second round of funding to continue or be professionally packaged for possible acquisition. The decision was made to attempt to sell the company, and it was acquired two years later. While my executive position did not carry over to the acquiring company, thanks to my dear friend and then company director, General Paul Harvey, I received severance pay of one year's salary.

I was soon hired for an outside counsel position with a

private gaming company based in Houston. I frequently commuted from Las Vegas to Houston and continued with my career pursuits in gaming for the next year. During this time, David also moved to southern Nevada after he graduated from high school in Florida, and we lived together in Henderson.

When the house that David had loved and grown up in since he was five weeks old was sold after the divorce, Lillie moved out of state to pursue a career opportunity in education. David wanted to live with me, and I felt a lot of parental responsibility to guide him in a positive and productive manner. I was also very protective, if not overprotective, of his emotions. As sad as I had been about being divorced, I was always more concerned about the impact the divorce would have on my children.

In 2007, I was approached by a law firm, Howard & Howard, that was opening a Las Vegas office for their nationwide firm based in the suburbs of Detroit, Michigan. They were seeking a gaming law specialist and someone who had an industry following. As I had been doing some outside work for clients in between jobs and had a modest book of business to bring with me, I was offered a position as a shareholder/partner in the firm. I had never thought about working at a major firm, but it was a new and enjoyable experience. I was able to market to new clients in Las Vegas as well as travel internationally to seek foreign gaming companies' engagement in domestic legal services.

As with most law firms, a partner's ongoing association with the organization was based on production. Although I had a foundational base of business to become an incoming partner in the firm, two years into my association with Howard & Howard, the 2009 recession hit the nation. Gaming was not a priority for the American people, and most gaming companies were trying to manage their costs and just stay open, rather than invest in product development and new business ventures. One day, I was invited to lunch by my friend and client Joe Cole, who was the owner and CEO of Cole Industries, a gaming cabinet fabricator in North Las Vegas.

After some general discussion about life and family, Joe asked, "Do you want to continue billing me by the hour?"

"What do you have in mind, Joe?"

"I want you to consider working for me full-time."

"Really? You're looking for an in-house counsel?"

He smiled and said, "No, I was actually hoping you might consider accepting the position of president of Cole Industries."

I was shocked yet humbled. After a few moments to collect my thoughts, I said, "I am honored by the thought and opportunity, but I just don't have the skills or experience to manage a metal fabrication company with a workforce of one hundred employees."

His response was impactful. "Glenn, I don't care what degrees you have or what experience you may or may not have. I like the way you treat people, and I trust you. That is all that matters to me."

I had known Joe for some years and always appreciated his knowledge and intelligence in developing a successful private manufacturing business. I also knew from my experience and the experience of others who had worked with Joe that he was a man of his word. Our values aligned; he always said to me that the most important assets of his company were his employees.

I wanted to work with Joe and expand my knowledge of how manufacturing businesses needed to operate to be successful in the gaming industry. After we discussed specifics and time frames, I was able to provide reasonable notice to my firm and accept my new employment with Cole Industries.

Cole Industries was a family-owned business and major gaming cabinet fabricator and provider in the US gaming industry. While their product was proven and tested, the company lacked a larger portfolio of customers to rely upon for its revenue base. My close friend and colleague Craig Askins, who was the new vice president of business development, and I suggested to Joe that there was a vast and mostly untouched market of gaming customers in Europe, Central and South America, Asia, and Australia. Many of these gaming companies were seeking to introduce their products into the US market, and Cole Industries could provide both a domestic source of gaming cabinets for their software and a way to easily drop-ship their final product to their US-based customers. We began to expand our customer portfolio and transform Cole Industries into an internationally recognized supplier of gaming cabinetry. Craig and I also began to exhibit the products of Cole Industries at the ICE Gaming exposition in London; the Asia G2E Gaming Expo in Macau; and the SAGSE gaming expos in Panama City, Panama, and Buenos Aires.

By 2011, David had returned to Boca Raton to complete his college education at Lynn University, and I rented a townhouse that he and I lived in when I was not in Las Vegas for business. So I had the flexibility of commuting for work purposes either way.

Cole Industries also had a strategic partner based in Taiwan known as Kepro, which fabricated gaming cabinets and other metal products for the electronic gaming machine and other industries. Joe asked me to travel to Taiwan to meet with Kepro's general manager, Mason Peng, to see how we could work together.

Before the trip, Joe suggested I approach Kepro with a standard proposition where each of our companies supported the sales of the other in the various regions of the world closer in proximity to our respective factories, where we would not compete with each other. In return for sales support, a commission would be paid for referral customers. When we sat down in Mason's corporate offices and began drinking cups of green tea together, I sensed this approach wouldn't work.

Instead, I suggested to Mason that our time might be better spent by working together under one corporate umbrella. Within a few months thereafter, an agreement was reached between Cole Industries and Kepro that created the new US corporate entity known as Cole Kepro International. We worked as a team in markets rather than sharing separate commissions for referred sales opportunities.

I greatly enjoyed the opportunity to help grow the company and test my international business and marketing skills—skills I was unaware I had. My international travels were not only successful but also memorable from cultural and business perspectives. I enjoyed learning about different cultures and how these differences manifested themselves in daily life and business in a foreign country. In business meetings, I learned cultural subtleties. For example, in most of Asia, it is customary to present a business card to the other party by holding it, face up, with the thumb and first finger of both hands at its lower corners. Also, in Japanese business culture, a response of yes doesn't necessarily mean yes. It would commonly be considered a statement relative to "I heard you." I learned how to be sensitive to and respectful of foreign culture and customs—very important in order to be successful on a business level and appreciated on a personal level. I continue to apply this acquired knowledge and understanding in my personal and business life.

For my business trips to Asia, I always tried to extend my trip a few personal days to explore this new world far from home. My travels took me to Thailand, Myanmar (previously known as Burma), China, Taiwan, and Japan. I also frequented Vietnam and ultimately invested in a travel agency based in Hanoi. I learned much about the Vietnam War and the other side of the story from my friends and colleagues in Vietnam who had lived through it (though they referred to it as "the American War"). It was so interesting to connect the dots of what we were told about the war from our own government while growing up during that era to what the reality was when considering the facts and opinions of those who lived through the war in their own backyard.

In early 2011, I was on a business trip in Birmingham, Alabama, with Joe and Craig. We were meeting with the president of a Mississippi-based gaming company who was interested in a joint venture. This would be an opportunity to market our gaming cabinets to new and emerging game software companies based largely in Europe.

Toward the late afternoon of our first day in Birmingham, I received a phone call from my father. His voice was very subdued. "Glenn, I just got a phone call from California. Claudia died. Please come home."

I was in disbelief. My sister had been temporarily living in Los Angeles to assist one of her daughters through some legal and medical issues. I immediately called my stepfather in Las Vegas and asked him to confirm the news. Claudia had indeed passed away, but the cause was unknown. I went to the lobby, shared the news with my colleagues, and began looking for a flight to Las Vegas to be with my family.

I sat in my hotel room in Birmingham overnight and hardly slept. When the sun began to rise the next morning, I traveled by car to Atlanta and boarded a flight to Fort Lauderdale so I could pick up a suit at home to wear at the funeral. I then boarded another flight to Las Vegas and arrived late in the afternoon. I went into an emotionally numb robotic mode knowing that a difficult time with much emotion and responsibility would lie ahead.

When I arrived at my mother's house in Las Vegas, there was mostly silence despite the gathering of friends and family. When someone passes away after a long life or a challenge with serious illness, you have some time to say goodbye, prepare yourself emotionally, and recognize the good life that the departed lived. When there is an accident or sudden death, it becomes a totally unscripted event coupled with grief and shock.

As soon as I could, I went into a side room with my mother, Kap, and my cousin Michael. I asked them what had happened to my sister. What they knew was that she had apparently tripped and hit her head on a windowsill in her grandson's bedroom, dying of a brain hemorrhage. What was strange was that she had packed up her belongings in suitcases and was planning to return home to Las Vegas later that day. There was something in this explanation that just didn't sound right to me and some family members, and our suspicions were raised.

While Claudia was being transported to Las Vegas from Los Angeles for her funeral, Kap and I discussed options with my mother. We could proceed with the funeral and see Claudia laid to rest without confirmation of how she passed away, or we could consider another option. After much internal discussion, we decided to retain the services of a private forensic pathologist to perform an autopsy on Claudia at the funeral home prior to the actual funeral. I suggested to my mother that some simple pathology could be performed, such as blood testing and analysis, but I am sure she sensed what would actually be conducted. My mother was in despair with the sudden loss of her daughter, and the idea of having an autopsy performed on her body was so uncomfortable and hurtful for her to consider.

We delayed the funeral by one day and told friends and family there was a delay in transporting her to Las Vegas from Los Angeles. I asked the funeral director to view Claudia's body and inform me of any bruises to her head or body as a result of the purported fall and head injury she had sustained. Claudia was a heavyset woman toward the end of her life, and she bruised easily, but there were no bruises noted to her head or on her body.

The autopsy was then conducted by the forensic pathologist, though it would be a number of weeks until an official report would be issued to the family. It is so terrible and tragic to lose a sibling, and it was even worse to witness my parents sitting arm in arm with each other in total grief, shock, and despair at their own child's funeral. This was the worst of times, but I went through it moment by moment, just taking each next step forward as best I could.

Eight weeks later, my mother and Kap were visiting me and David in South Florida. During their visit, I received a call from the forensic pathologist. She shared that her findings were concerning and she had contacted the Los Angeles County Medical Examiner to open an inquiry. The forensic report read that Claudia had died from a lethal combination of two drugs: fentanyl, an opioid, and Lexapro, an antidepressant. The findings conflicted with the story that we had been told. Her death certificate indicated she had died of a heart attack, which also conflicted with the information we had been initially told about the cause of her death. While she wore prescribed fentanyl time-released patches on her body for pain suppression, she would not have overdosed on the medication unless the patches were opened and the contents had been either ingested or injected into her system.

I began to automatically move into the role of amateur investigator, making a list of every person who had been around Claudia near her time of death. I traced her online footprint, noting that she was actively posting on Facebook about her favorite band, Aerosmith, at 7:30 a.m. that day and that she was clearly coherent that morning until the time of her death, approximately 12:30 p.m. I kept detailed notes of everything that I learned and contacted law enforcement officials in Los Angeles, asking for an audience with their detectives in order to support opening a full investigation into Claudia's death. I didn't hear back.

I then spoke with the Los Angeles County coroner, Ed Winter, who was known as the "coroner to the stars" due to the many investigations he had conducted following the suspicious deaths of famous entertainers in Los Angeles over the years. Mr. Winter informed me that the detectives had not contacted him following my repeated attempts to seek the opening of a criminal inquiry. He apologized for the inaction of LAPD Homicide but said he had no control over what cases they would investigate. In closing, he suggested I go with my first impressions of what may have occurred. But that wasn't enough for me.

My cousin Sky had been a noted criminal defense attorney in Miami for many years. When I expressed to him my frustration in dealing with the detectives, he stated from his experience that detectives aren't necessarily the perfect professional types depicted in movies and television shows. His opinion was that many detectives are not very motivated unless the evidence before them is clear cut.

Following my many requests for a personal audience with law enforcement and being lobbied by a close friend of mine, I was finally granted an opportunity for a meeting with detectives of the LAPD Homicide division in West Los Angeles. I entered the investigation room, which was similar to what one would expect. Two detectives, a table with a few chairs, nothing decorating the stark walls, and a cold atmosphere greeted me. I shared my thoughts and concerns, including all my notes about the events that had transpired. The meeting concluded ninety minutes later.

While I would receive correspondence now and then from the detectives at LAPD Homicide about delays in their investigation due to other pressing criminal situations they had to investigate first, ultimately, no further inquiry or investigation was ever conducted, and the case remains open. The shock waves of this horrific event continued to shake my family's emotional foundation for years. Claudia was sixty-three years old.

Claudia was the mother of three children, and she worked at times with our father at Games of Nevada and in other gaming and amusement business opportunities that our father made possible for her to pursue, just as I did. She was the Nevada distributor for Atari and operated an amusement machine location known as the Mighty Marble Machine as well as the second Honest John's Casino. Her life wasn't perfect and she struggled at times, living a fast and mostly unhealthy lifestyle.

It seemed both my siblings were burning the candle at both ends. Tragically, they both died so young. I always thought that the progression of life meant that when my parents were no longer with me, my siblings would be there to continue as a family and share common memories of our childhoods and life together. But life doesn't always work out that way. I still feel this emptiness often, especially during the holiday seasons, and certain places we lived in or visited in the past bring back memories of the way my family life used to be.

I was still processing my shock about Claudia's death and attempting my own investigation when Joe Cole decided to sell his majority interest in Cole Kepro to a private equity company. Upon acquiring this equity position, the private equity group installed their new CEO. When I met him, I was informed that I was now president of the company in title only. My name and good reputation in the gaming industry would be helpful for the new owners in the further growth and development of the company. I would continue with the company as "president" for public consumption, but I no longer had any management function within the business. This was yet another big disappointment during a very difficult year.

I continued to engage in international business development as I had in the past, but I was told I would no longer have an office on the premises. It was apparent to me that the new owners wanted to establish new leadership at the factory without my presence or any possible or perceived interference. Since my son had returned to Boca Raton to attend college, I decided to work remotely and return to South Florida, which had always felt like home.

CHAPTER 18

A Life Chapter Closes

I continued working for Cole Kepro for the next five years and commuted between South Florida and Las Vegas every two weeks. I also engaged in many international marketing efforts and traveled overseas to attend more gaming trade expositions and international gaming law conferences. The world of gaming was changing as online games became more prominent, which eventually would leave the gaming cabinet industry in much less market demand.

In December 2012, my father spent some time in a rehabilitation facility following a pacemaker implantation. I visited him when I was in Las Vegas, and he looked good and strong again, insistent on leaving the rehab center and returning home. When I next visited him at his home in January and early February 2013, he was beginning to look very frail to me. I never knew if the next visit with my father would be the last. As I was leaving his bedroom on my last visit, I said to him, "I love you, Dad."

He responded, "I know you do."

I traveled home to South Florida and the following day received a phone call from my niece, Robyn, Claudia's younger daughter, informing me that her brother Keith was not conscious and an ambulance had just arrived at his home in North Las Vegas. I asked her to keep me informed. She called me back later to tell me that Keith had passed away. Keith was a wonderful young man with a beautiful heart. Unfortunately, he also lived an unhealthy lifestyle and died way too soon, at forty-five years old.

I had to break the news on the phone to my father. I told him I would travel back to Las Vegas for the funeral, which was scheduled for that coming Friday. I planned to visit with him afterward, as he did not have the energy to leave the house and attend the funeral. On Friday morning, I was back in Las Vegas, getting dressed to attend Keith's funeral, when I received a voice message from my stepmother, Zola, saying that my father had just been transported by ambulance to Valley Hospital. "Please get here as quickly as you can," she said.

"How is he?" I asked Zola as I hurried into the emergency room.

"I don't know," she said. "No one will tell me anything."

I finally approached one of the doctors on call and said it was important to see how my father was doing as I needed to be at my nephew's funeral in an hour. I was thinking the worst and considering another meaning for the term "doubleheader." The doctor walked us back to the triage area of the emergency room and softly said, "The gentleman has expired."

I was speechless. My first impulse was to call his primary care doctor, and then I realized there was nothing his doctor could do for him anymore. Zola asked to see him one more time and wanted me to go with her. I walked behind the closed screen into the triage area, kissed my father on his forehead, and said goodbye for the last time.

I made sure that Zola had someone to be with her at home

and left for Keith's funeral. On the way, I called my mother and Kap as well as a couple of other relatives who would be attending Keith's funeral, to share with them what had just happened. I don't know how I managed to be coherent and stable during Keith's funeral. Maybe I was in shock and simply numb, but I was able to place my emotions for my father on hold. I went through what I needed to address in a robotic way, just as I'd done when Claudia unexpectedly passed away two years earlier.

Instead of spending time with my father as we had planned, I went to the cemetery office and arranged his funeral for the following Monday. My world seemed to stand still. My father had such a great influence and impact on every moment of my adult life. I would miss him so incredibly much. My father lived a full life to the age of ninety.

His memorial service was attended by more than one hundred friends and colleagues, and his grave site was right next to that of Keith and Claudia. I prepared a eulogy and, despite being so emotionally spent, somehow found the energy to make a meaningful pronouncement about my father and his life. It was well received by those in attendance, and I was proud to speak before them as Mickey's son.

I assumed I would be entering into a grieving period for a significant amount of time after my father's passing and his funeral. However, I also realized that my father had lived a complex and sometimes contentious life, and I sensed storm clouds developing in the distance. Our personal accountant in Los Angeles was a wonderful man named Ronald Koblin. Ron was not only our accountant; we truly cared about each other and were treated as members of each other's families.

I began to recall a conversation that Ron had with me some years earlier. Ron said to me in a soft voice, "Glenn, one day when your dad is no longer here, it's going to be fireworks." Ron must have been psychically sensitive.

I had barely regained my footing when, a few months later, I was working for Cole Kepro and exhibiting their products at the G2E Global Gaming Expo in Las Vegas. I was in front of our exhibit stand at the expo when someone approached me and asked, "Are you Glenn Wichinsky?"

I smiled and said, "Yes, I'm Glenn."

This individual then handed me a stack of documents and said, "This is for you."

I was shocked to realize I'd been served with a summons and civil complaint filed by Zola. The basis of the suit was estate litigation—Zola was disputing who should receive what, and I was served because I was executor of my father's estate. To make matters worse and to be even more hurtful, she also had me named personally as a defendant in the action. Without the need to go into personal detail, suffice it to say that my father lived a full life—many lives within the same one. He had made a provision in his estate planning to someone who had been special in his life for many years, and by doing so, he triggered rage, anger, and resentment in his wife.

While I understood her anger and hurtful feelings, I could not change his will as she demanded. I could only administer it in the way he had expressed his wishes to his estate attorney. While she had every right to be mad at my father, I was deeply hurt by the fact that she would target her anger and rage against me. My father used to offer the remark: "When you dance, you pay the fiddler." When you stray in your relationship, you pay the price. In this instance, by being executor of his estate, I had stepped into my father's shoes and was paying the price for his hurtful and unthinking actions.

During the court proceedings, Zola contacted the Nevada Gaming Control Board and requested they issue her a temporary gaming license so she could continue to operate my father's company, Advanced Gaming Technology. She told the regulators that she was an integral part of the business and needed to have the authority to operate it. The fact of the matter was that she was never involved in my father's gaming businesses, and I doubted she had ever set foot into his offices in over forty years. Despite this, a temporary gaming license was issued, and it effectively tied my hands in trying to manage the estate.

I contacted the deputy attorney general of the Nevada Gaming Control Board and requested their assistance. The immediate response was that this was a civil matter and not within the province or jurisdiction of the state gaming regulators. A couple of months later, my retained estate defense attorneys received a letter from one of Zola's attorneys. The letter stated that Zola would allow the estate the use of her temporary gaming license in return for compensation. It is legally prohibited to offer the use of your granted gaming license to another in return for compensation.

I immediately contacted the chair of the Nevada Gaming Control Board, informed him of what had transpired, and provided a copy of the proposal from Zola and her attorney. Within a month, her temporary gaming license was revoked, and I was then able to begin a necessary liquidation of the business assets of the estate. The business was essentially dormant, had no employees, and could not be a functional business without my father. It was his ideas and projects, his personality and standing that made all his businesses successful.

The estate litigation continued for almost two years until I was finally successful. It was a terrible time to live through, and ultimately, after all this pain and suffering by everyone involved, Zola passed away a month after judgment was rendered against her. It is difficult for me to balance my thoughts and emotions about Zola at times. I knew, loved, and respected her from the time I first met her when I was thirteen years old. I had also felt the love and caring she showed to me, my wife, and my children. It was not easy to believe that what ultimately mattered to her was money. She had even taken my father's small black address book, called his business associates, and insinuated that he stole her money and that I changed the will and misappropriated estate funds.

It was the worst feeling in the world to be accused of something that was not true and then have to defend myself from the allegations while I was mourning the loss of my father. For my personal well-being, I had to distance myself from business and personal relationships that had been influenced by Zola's baseless opinions. I even felt physically threatened after an offensive phone call received from a family member whom Zola had contacted.

I still haven't fully worked through this additional nightmare chapter in my life. What a waste of time, money, energy, and misdirected emotions. But, by the end of December 2015, with the court cases closed, I was finally able to begin grieving the loss of my father.

CHAPTER 19

Grieving and New Revelations

When we lose a loved one, we often reflect on the moments that we spent together and have some remorse for not having learned more about their life. This is how I felt about losing my father. While we did not develop a stronger bond until I moved to Las Vegas after graduating college, I never asked him what his childhood was like, whether he had engaged in sports or hobbies when he was young, or how his life had unfolded in the years before I truly knew him.

I was respectful of the fact that he seemingly did not want to discuss his childhood memories with me. All I knew was that he had grown up in a poor family as one of nine children, all of whom worked hard for every dollar. I was not comfortable asking him about his mother and father, as his father was abusive to his mother, and she was eventually placed in a state institution when my father was around eight years old.

We never spoke about his relationship with and twelve-year

marriage to my mother, as he was not a good husband to her; she asked for a divorce in the late 1950s, a time when it was more common for a housewife to put up with her husband's indiscretions than to hire an attorney and leave him.

I was curious how he became so successful in life on his path to being a gaming executive and minority interest equity owner in the famous Sands Hotel. I knew only that his humble beginnings included operating a route of pinball machines and jukeboxes in the Catskill Mountains and starting out at the Sands from the bottom of the ladder. He had done everything from being a slot machine mechanic to a pit boss overseeing many of the table games. I assumed I would never learn the answers to my many questions.

Some months after my father had passed, I was walking through a bookstore in Boca Raton perusing books related to gaming and Las Vegas. I would often open the new publications, about Las Vegas or the gaming industry, and go to their index to see if I recognized any familiar names of people whom I had met in Las Vegas when I was younger. I noticed a new release of a book entitled *Hit Me! Fighting the Las Vegas Mob by the Numbers* by Danielle Gomes and Jay Bonansinga. The nonfiction account explored some of the many investigations that Ms. Gomes's late father, Dennis Gomes, had conducted during his career as an agent and investigator with the Nevada Gaming Control Board.

I opened the book to the index and scrolled through the names. When I got to the letter *W*, I stopped and froze for a moment. There was a reference in the index to my father, Michael Wichinsky. Not only was there a reference, but there was a complete chapter written about him. I immediately purchased the book and went to my car in the parking lot, where I read the whole chapter with astonishment.

In the early 1970s, Special Agent Dennis Gomes conducted an investigation of Bally Manufacturing Company, for whom my father was the southern Nevada distributor. At the time, Bally was an emerging slot machine manufacturer owned by members of organized crime. His investigation led to my father's distributorship business, his personal and business associations, and his business relationships with those whom gaming regulators would view as being of an unsavory character.

There were references to my father's travels and whereabouts after his divorce from my mother in 1957 and investigative records of information received from informants. At the end of the chapter, Ms. Gomes concluded that my father was an "admitted mobster." I was outraged! I knew that my father had to rub elbows with people at a time when most hotels and casinos in Las Vegas were owned and controlled by members of organized crime. However, to paint my father, who was recently deceased, as a mobster and place him in a fictional role that might align with criminals in *The Godfather* or *Casino* was a mischaracterization of who he was as I knew him.

I sent Ms. Gomes an email expressing my concerns. She was kind to promptly respond in a sincere manner. Ms. Gomes explained to me that the information contained in the book was based on the many documented investigations her father had conducted during his years working for the Nevada gaming regulators. She also shared with me that her depiction of my father was just one of "a moment in time," and that her father had often commented to her that he viewed my father as a nice man who just had associations with some bad people. Danielle, as I would come to know her on a first-name basis, knew that what I read may have been hurtful to digest, but she offered me a special gift that would become the catalyst for this book.

All her father's investigative records were maintained under seal at the University of Nevada, Las Vegas, Special Collections and Archives, but Danielle offered to get me access to the investigative files that pertained to my father. I would be allowed to review the information but not to copy or reproduce any documents. I spent three hours reviewing numerous files of information about my father, tracing as far back as his military records during World War II, his associations and activities in the late 1950s and '60s, and even a very detailed FBI Strike Force report on his whereabouts and activities. Afterward, I wrote back to Danielle, thanking her for the opportunity to review this sensitive information and also for her discretion in the information that she had decided to publish.

I began to dig deeper into his history and informally interview friends and associates who knew my father from those earlier days and felt comfortable having a frank discussion. Between what I learned from the sealed investigative information and the interviews I conducted, I began to paint a picture of the amazing and clandestine life that my father had once led—a life that he never shared with me, for my own protection.

CHAPTER 20

Retrospective: My Father in the Late 1950s and '60s

Though what I've shared thus far in this book has been about my life and recollections, there is another story underneath. I am going to rewind the story back to the beginning and share the parts of my father's life that I have uncovered with a bit more clarity.

After my parents' divorce in 1957, I heard from my father every Sunday when he would call us from Las Vegas to say hello. He occasionally saw me, Claudia, and Steven when he traveled through New York to visit colleagues and family in Hurleyville. In the general way of children, I wasn't that interested in what he did for a living at the time. However, he always made time to take us to dinner with him when visiting.

When we moved to North Miami Beach, this continued, with occasional visits and dinners. He would also spend time with some of his old friends who were originally from the Catskills and see his brother, my uncle Nate, who lived nearby.

Upon reading the chapter about my father in *Hit Me!*, I began piecing together the various parts of the puzzle of my father's life that I never knew. Special Agent Gomes investigated allegations in 1971 that my father's distribution company, Bally Sales Corporation of Nevada, was an arm of or front for the Genovese crime family, which effectively controlled and operated Bally Manufacturing Company in Chicago. During the investigation into Bally Sales, Mr. Gomes was able to enlist the testimony of a paid government informant, an attorney named Herbert Itkin. Mr. Itkin was familiar with the activities of many individuals who were associated with organized crime. The informant was asked if he knew my father, to which he responded that he did. He further stated that my father was "a nice guy," and that he had been in Cuba with my father. When asked if my father was associated with the Mob, the informant responded: "Oh yeah. He's close with some of the top bosses. I mean, he's not a bad guy, but he's in business with some of the worst."

Post-divorce, my father was invited to spend a month in Havana at the Riviera Hotel. During this time, Mr. Itkin linked my father, both personally and in business, with members of the organized crime families, including the Lucchese and Genovese crime families as well as Meyer Lansky. I once asked my father if he had known Meyer Lansky. His response was "I never met the old man." I now believed otherwise.

In recent years, Myron Sugerman, being "the last of the Jewish gangsters," shared with me that not only was my uncle Nate associated with the activities of Murder, Inc. in the Catskills in the 1930s as I had suspected but he was actually "the connection guy in the Catskills for Meyer Lansky and for Murder, Inc."

Considered the "patriarch" of the Wichinsky family, Uncle Nate seemingly and indirectly introduced his kid brother,

Mickey, into this path during his early career, connecting him to a world of intrigue. I understood that Uncle Nate felt responsible for my father after their challenging childhood and probably wanted a better life for him than being a driver of a family bakery truck or operating a seasonal pinball machine and jukebox route. My father once asked Claudia to please honor his wishes after he died: He would never be laid to rest in Hurleyville. Clearly, he wanted to leave his childhood behind him.

Back in Havana in the late 1950s, the Mob was concerned about the safety of their assets in Cuba as Fidel Castro marched through the country with his revolutionaries. Among their prized assets were the slot machines operating in their Havana casinos. There was no doubt that Castro would close the casinos and destroy any gambling equipment left on the island. My father was apparently assigned the task of seeing that most of the slot machines in casinos operated by some organized crime families be exported before Castro and his revolutionary army rolled into Havana. I was told that my father was successful in moving a large quantity of these Havana-based slot machines to the Colony Club in London, a casino owned and operated by Meyer Lansky.

With the fall of Cuba in 1959, the Mob then turned their attention back to illegal gambling markets in the United States as well as the growing legal gambling and casino market operating in Nevada. My father was then living in Las Vegas and working at two jobs to support himself and his family. He began working at the Sands Hotel and Casino after being referred to the hotel by connected associates. The Sands, like other hotel casinos, was Mob-owned and fronted by individuals who could receive gaming license approval to operate the gaming locations. My father began as a slot mechanic at the Sands in the late 1950s, worked up through the casino as a dealer, then a pit boss, and eventually was able to purchase a 2 percent equity position (which he referred to as "two points") in the Sands.

At the same time, my father was operating a small gaming company in Las Vegas known as Frontier Coin. During this period a very large and prosperous illegal gambling and casino market was operating in the United Kingdom. My understanding is that my father was able to acquire hundreds of used mechanical slot machines that were warehoused across the United States, refurbish them, and ship containers of them to illegal operators in London and its vicinity.

My father hired two gentlemen, Moe and his nephew Jimmy, to make local inquiries and search various warehouses across the United States to locate used slot machines, as they were illegal to operate in most of the country. My father gave them a large amount of cash with only one instruction: *Come back with truckloads of slot machines for refurbishing.* The monies that funded this effort were arranged by a partnership between the Lucchese and Genovese crime families. Shipment was to be made to a Mob individual named Herbie Katz in England, who was a Lucchese family associate. The venture was successful for all concerned until England legalized casino gambling in private clubs in the early 1960s.

By the mid-1960s, Bally Manufacturing began producing the first electromechanical slot machines, and Bally soon became the market share leader of slot machines throughout the world. After some false starts and needed modifications, their styling and operation became an industry standard. What also made them revolutionary was their ability to pay out hundreds of coins in jackpots by using the incorporated hopper payout unit in the game cabinet. As my father introduced Bally to the hopper technology, he was, in return, rewarded with the payment of ongoing royalties following the granting of his southern Nevada distributorship for Bally slot machines.

My father left the Sands Hotel in the late 1960s when it was purchased by the Summa Corporation, owned by aviation magnate Howard Hughes. My father continued selling Bally slot machines through his southern Nevada distributorship as he faced fierce competition from Si Redd, the Bally distributor for northern Nevada and the future founder of International Game Technology (IGT). It also didn't help the situation that my father's company, Bally Sales Corporation of Nevada, was raided by Agent Gomes in 1971, and my father and his company had been placed under a higher level of scrutiny by the Nevada Gaming Control Board. Ultimately, the bosses at Bally Manufacturing liked the sales and game placement numbers they saw being generated by Mr. Redd and instructed my father to sell his distributorship to Mr. Redd in the early 1970s.

Following the sale of his Bally distributorship, my father began to remove himself from business activities on the Las Vegas Strip, took a lower business and personal profile in his activities, distanced himself from prior business associations, and became a sole proprietor of his own independent gaming company, Games of Nevada, which opened in 1972. This was about the time that I began to visit him every summer and ultimately moved to Las Vegas to work with him following my graduation from the University of Miami in 1974.

By this time, my father no longer lived the busy public and business life that he had enjoyed while being a hotel executive on the Las Vegas Strip for many years. He now put in long hours to develop his own independent business and new game prototypes. Following occasional dinners out with friends and family, he returned home early and watched television. I don't recall him going to any hotels, casinos, or restaurants on the Strip, and my feeling is that he wanted to remove himself from the past and from most of his old associations.

When Uncle Nate occasionally stayed in Las Vegas for a protracted period of time, he lived in a bungalow or cottage at the Aladdin Hotel. Uncle Nate had his own old circle of hard-line associates whom my father wanted nothing to do with. When I asked my father if he was going to visit Uncle Nate on the Strip with his friends, my father said he had no plans of being around "Natey's friends." They were apparently hardcore mobsters.

I believe that after Bally Manufacturing essentially forced my father to sell his Bally distributorship to Si Redd, he just wanted to be his own person, provide for his family, and live a simpler life. He hardly ever discussed events with me that preceded the year 1972. I also believe that as much as he wanted his son to be with him and to get to know him after the years apart, he didn't want me actually working in the business. He just wanted me near him. I can understand that now. Had he not sheltered me from the truth over all these years, I might have had difficulties achieving what I have in life. His past and the associations he'd had could have been a much bigger burden on me.

My father operated his business as a sole proprietorship, without any of the legal protections afforded to one when operating as a corporate entity. He believed in trusting people, was generally nonjudgmental, and often conducted business based only on a handshake. I was always impressed how he never dismissed employees at Games of Nevada unless he was first able to find them another job elsewhere. He deeply cared about others and tried to be of help whenever he could.

Conclusion

In the years since my father passed away and all the family-related drama ended, life for me has become peaceful and very reflective. I learned a lot about life and business from my father, mostly from my personal observation. I followed in his footsteps by engaging in worldwide business travel, learning to be creative, and not passing judgment on the actions or decisions of others. Like my father, I always place my family first and foremost in my life.

I have been involved in many aspects of the regulated global gaming industry for over forty years and have engaged in such pursuits as casino management, acting as a gaming executive and general counsel for a public company, finding my talent in conducting international business development for my employers or clients, exploring Vietnam and helping establish a concierge travel agency based in Hanoi, creating business joint ventures and partnerships domestically and internationally, being a speaker and moderator at professional gaming law forums and conferences, and becoming an adjunct professor of gaming law at my law school alma mater, the University of the Pacific, McGeorge School of Law.

Following the passing of Steven in 1995, Claudia in 2011, my nephew Keith, and my father in 2013, and later, my stepfather, Kap, and my mother, my family circle has become very small. I have many wonderful memories and some challenging ones as well from my past with family, but I do think of all of them with much love and affection.

I have since gotten remarried to a wonderful woman named Hebe. Hebe has two loving daughters, and in addition to my own son and daughter, my family has grown again.

My father is remembered by many friends and colleagues in the gaming industry as a good and caring man. He had his challenges beginning in his childhood and navigated them as best he knew how, based on the upbringing he had in Hurleyville. He was good to me, my siblings, and countless individuals whom he helped throughout his life. Prior to his passing, my father was awarded the Lifetime Achievement Award for his fifty years of service in the Nevada gaming industry by the State of Nevada Gaming Commission.

I once asked him how he might want to be remembered. He responded, "I would like to be remembered as a good person who lived a full life."

I continue to meet people who knew my father and want to share with me their impressions of him as being "a good person," "a lovely person," "a peach of a man," and "a caring person." People who knew him well would also remark to me that I was "the apple of his eye." Myron Sugerman, author of *The Chronicles of the Last Jewish Gangster*, told me that "as far as your father is concerned, a piece of his greatness was that he swam in the same ocean with sharks and yet the sharks were smart enough to recognize that Mickey Wichinsky was of a very special character and to be respected."

Most of the gaming machines and prototypes that he developed were donated by his estate to the gaming collection at the Nevada State Museum in Las Vegas. As my father would say, "This is for posterity." I recently established a scholarship in his name at my former law school to honor his life and thank him for believing in me, supporting me, and assisting me while I attended law school as well as for the exciting and fulfilling professional career that ensued as a result. The scholarship is known as the Michael "Mickey" Wichinsky Gaming Law Endowed Scholarship. It financially assists law students at the McGeorge School of Law who express an academic interest in pursuing the field of gaming law.

As his health was declining and prior to his passing, I asked my father if he would consider having a book written about his life. He responded that if he did, he would need to wear a bulletproof vest.

"Dad, those people are gone and in the past," I said.

"No, they aren't."

It may be true that it wouldn't have been safe for my father to tell his story. So now that he is gone, I have told it in his honor.

Acknowledgments

Thank you to Sara Addicott and her dedicated editing and publishing staff at Girl Friday Productions in Seattle for their guidance and support in finalizing and publishing this book, and for advising and educating me on the finer points of "storytelling."

Thank you to Mark Weinstein and his staff at Kevin Anderson & Associates in New York City for their initial editing and critical review of my manuscript and for their guidance as I sought a successful path in the vast world of publishing.

I'd like to thank Mona Houck for providing her professional services and conducting a prepublication legal review of my manuscript.

My daughter, Laura, has always loved and supported me in my decisions in life. She constructively challenged me not to round the corners in sharing my story and life events but to be deep, direct, and fully open to the readers as to what events had truly transpired in my life and how they affected me.

My son, David, has also always loved and respected his dad unconditionally in life.

Thank you to my wife, Hebe, and her daughters, Juli and Mili, for their love, caring, and support of me in all that I pursue and seek to achieve in my life.

Thank you to Lillie Wichinsky and her sister, Sherry Holden, for reviewing my initial work and offering their reflections and comments to assist me in providing the best depiction of the events that transpired and for joining me in much of this journey.

I'd like to thank my mother, Ann, who sadly departed this life before this book was finalized. She shared many personal stories of her life and family with me and always provided me with love, caring, and advice to overcome the many challenges I faced along the way.

Thank you to my cousins Ceil, Stacey, and Michael Rosen, who, with their love, reviewed my work and greatly encouraged me throughout this publishing adventure.

I'd like to thank my dear friends Sam and Hilda Silver, who reviewed the initial draft of my manuscript and offered their thoughts and revisions for a work they believed to be worth developing and presenting for publication.

Thank you to my dear friend Robert Levy, who has shared this journey with me since we first met when we were both nine years old and who has always been emotionally supportive to me during life's challenges and endeavors.

Thank you to my "Brother Mark" Sarason, who lived a similar life to mine with the same father figure and who enjoys sharing stories together, past and present, with deep love, compassion, and affection.

Thank you to my close friends, Jonathan Kross (who once gifted me with a compass "to stay on course"), Steve Rubin, Sherri Rothberg, and Ken Rosenblat, who not only encouraged my work but also shared life's hurdles along our collective journeys.

I'd like to thank my annual baseball-trip buddies of many years who have expressed great interest in my "intriguing" story and in the publication of this book. Thank you, Bob, Sam, Abe, Larry, Bernie, Michael, Marshall, and Aaron!

My cousins Bonnie, Sky, and Sandy; my nieces Robyn and Dawn; and my friends Jody Kaufman, Shelli Miller, Craig Askins, Russell Mix, Sharon Walters, Bruce Merrin, and

Dennis Griffin, thank you for your interest, guidance, and support in achieving the publication of this work.

My sincere gratitude to Danielle Gomes and Myron Sugerman, without their input and sharing of important and revealing information and historical events, the writing of this book would not have been possible.

My thanks and appreciation to all my friends and family whom I may have inadvertently left out but whose assistance, friendship, and caring have made this personal endeavor possible.

About the Author

© Lee Smith

GLENN E. WICHINSKY is a gaming and business law attorney based in Boca Raton, Florida. He earned his bachelor's degree from the University of Miami and a juris doctor degree from the University of the Pacific, McGeorge School of Law, where he now teaches a course on gaming law and regulation as an adjunct professor. *Things Left Unsaid* is his first book.

www.ingramcontent.com/pod-product-compliance
Lightning Source LLC
Chambersburg PA
CBHW021146130626
46554CB00005B/1694